Rely on Thomas Cook as your travelling companion on your next trip and benefit from our unique heritage.

Thomas Cook **pocket** guides

IONIAN ISLANDS

Written by Christopher Catling, updated by Chris Deliso

Published by Thomas Cook Publishing
A division of Thomas Cook Tour Operations Limited
Company registration no. 3772199 England
The Thomas Cook Business Park, Unit 9, Coningsby Road,
Peterborough PE3 8SB, United Kingdom
Email: books@thomascook.com, Tel: +44 (0) 1733 416477
www.thomascookpublishing.com

Produced by Cambridge Publishing Management Limited
Burr Elm Court, Main Street, Caldecote CB23 7NU
www.cambridgepm.co.uk

ISBN: 978-1-84848-386-6

Series Editor: Karen Beaulah
Production/DTP: Steven Collins

Printed and bound in Spain by GraphyCems

CONTENTS

WHAT'S IN YOUR GUIDEBOOK?

Independent authors Impartial, up-to-date information from our travel experts who meticulously source local knowledge.

Experience Thomas Cook's 165 years in the travel industry and guidebook publishing enriches every word with expertise you can trust.

Travel know-how Thomas Cook has thousands of staff working around the globe, all living and breathing travel.

Editors Travel-publishing professionals, pulling everything together to craft a perfect blend of words, pictures, maps and design.

You, the traveller We deliver a practical, no-nonsense approach to information, geared to how you really use it.

Kefalonia's beautiful coastline

INTRODUCTION

Getting to know the Ionian Islands

Sarandë
Kalpakio
Kranea
Sidari
ALBANIA
20
Metsovo
Trygona
Eleousa
6
Paleokastritsa
Vrosina
Ioannina
GREECE
Corfu Town
Filiates
CORFU
6
Pramanta
25
Igoumenitsa
A2
Kalentzi
Paramythia
5
Lefkimmi
Glyki
Kerasona
Parga
Limni Pournia
Lakka
Loggos
Kanallaki
PAXOS
Gaios
21
Arta
ANTIPAXOS
Kompoti
Kanali
N
Krikellos
Amvrakikos Kolpos
Limni Kremaston
Preveza
42
Vonitsa
Amfilochia
Lefkas Town
Tryfos

MEGANISSI
KALAMOS
Vassiliki
Agrinio
Astakos
Ionian
Sea
Fiskardo
ITHAKA
Aitoliko
Katochi
KEFALONIA
Vathy
Mesolongi
Divarata
Patraikos Kolpos
Lixouri
Sami
Argostoli
Poros
Lakythra
Lapas
Skala
Varda
9
Kilini
Lechaina
Volimes
ZAKYNTHOS
Alykes
Gastouni
Amaliada
Zakynthos
Lithakia
Pyrgos
Large Town
Small Town
Motorway
Main Road
Minor Road
Airport
International Border
Ionian Islands
Ionian Islands
0
20 km
0
10 miles

Getting to know the Ionian Islands

The Ionian Islands have been celebrated since the time of Homer for their beautiful beaches, pine-clad mountains and dramatic coastlines. Rising out of the blue Ionian Sea, between Greece and Italy, these fertile islands are clothed in a tapestry of vineyards, olive groves, orchards and wheat fields, creating a patchwork of colour that sets them apart from the barren rocky terrain of many other Greek islands.

There are seven main islands in the Ionian group. Kefalonia is the largest, and together with neighbouring Lefkas is the most unspoilt and least developed for tourism. Zakynthos attracts many holidaymakers every year for its pretty villages, sandy beaches and wild nightlife. Tiny Paxos is a quiet haven for yachting and nature lovers, best reached from the pretty mainland town of Parga. Ithaka is the legendary home of Odysseus, hero of Homer's *Odyssey*, and makes an excellent day-trip destination from Lefkas. (Corfu to the north and Kythira to the south are not covered in this guide.)

SEA & MOUNTAINS

All the Ionian Islands are rugged and mountainous. Most of the fishing ports and farming villages cling to the sheltered eastern coasts, where many of the holiday resorts are also found. Travelling westward, the terrain becomes steeper and wilder, sometimes ending in spectacular cliffs. Despite this, some of the finest beaches are on the west coast, and it is well worth taking a trip by boat or overland to seek out some hidden sandy cove. The islands are also ideal for watersports. Northwesterly winds, rising in the afternoon, provide excellent conditions for sailing and windsurfing. Beneath the waves there's much to see too, and a glass-bottomed boat tour or scuba-diving course could be the highlight of your trip.

CASTLES & CULTURE

From the 14th century, the Ionian Islands were ruled by Venice, and sturdy castles and harbours were built to protect its shipping interests.

During the Byzantine era, painters escaped Turkish rule in Greece and came to the Ionian Islands to practise their art. Churches on the islands are filled with their glowing frescoes, painted in the distinctive style of the Ionian School.

NATURE

Walkers and cyclists flock to the Ionian Islands in the shoulder seasons for the quiet roads, good weather and lush countryside. Zakynthos and Kefalonia are the main nesting sites for loggerhead turtles during the June to September breeding season and, in order to protect these magnificent creatures, watersports and nocturnal activities are banned on the beaches they use.

A view of the village of Assos, Kefalonia

THE BEST OF THE IONIAN ISLANDS

TOP 10 ATTRACTIONS

- **Learn to windsurf in Vassiliki Bay** on Lefkas's south coast, which many say is the best windsurfing beach in Europe (see page 25).
- **Take a boat trip from Lefkas** to visit the offshore islands (see page 22).
- **Sunbathe at Myrtos beach**, the finest beach on Kefalonia and one of the best in Greece (see page 53).
- **Stroll around pretty Fiskardo on Kefalonia**, and stop for lunch in a taverna overlooking the millionaires' yachts in the harbour (see pages 50–51).
- **Explore Kefalonia's spectacular Drogarati Cave** and join a boat trip on the underground Melissani Lake (see pages 52–3).
- **Shop for rugs, bedspreads and tablecloths** at Volimes on Zakynthos (see page 80).

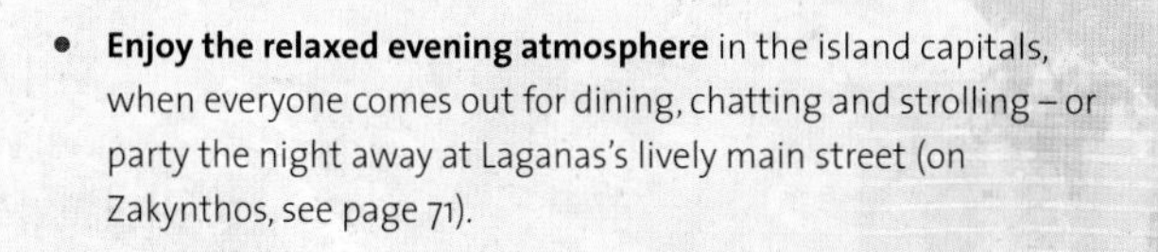

- **Enjoy the relaxed evening atmosphere** in the island capitals, when everyone comes out for dining, chatting and strolling – or party the night away at Laganas's lively main street (on Zakynthos, see page 71).

- **Marvel at the dazzling white cliffs** at Kampi and Shipwreck Bay on Zakynthos's west coast (see page 80).

- **Visit the charming mainland coastal town of Parga**, with its castle, houses tumbling down to the sea and good beaches (see page 89).

- **Wander around the picturesque harbours** of Lakka (see page 86) and Loggos (see page 84) on Paxos, and the deserted beaches and peaceful olive groves nearby.

Breathtaking view of Zakynthos's Shipwreck Bay

SYMBOLS KEY

The following symbols are used throughout this book:

ⓐ address ⓣ telephone ⓦ website address ⓔ email
opening times important

The following symbols are used on the maps:

i	information office	O	city
	post office	O	large town
	shopping	○	small town
	airport	■	point of interest
+	hospital		motorway
	police station		main road
	bus station		minor road
†	church		

❶ numbers denote featured cafés, restaurants & evening venues

RESTAURANT CATEGORIES

The symbol after the name of each restaurant listed in this guide indicates the price of a typical main course plus starter or dessert and drink for one person.

£ under €12 **££** €12–25 **£££** more than €25

The view over Parga Bay

RESORTS
The islands & excursions

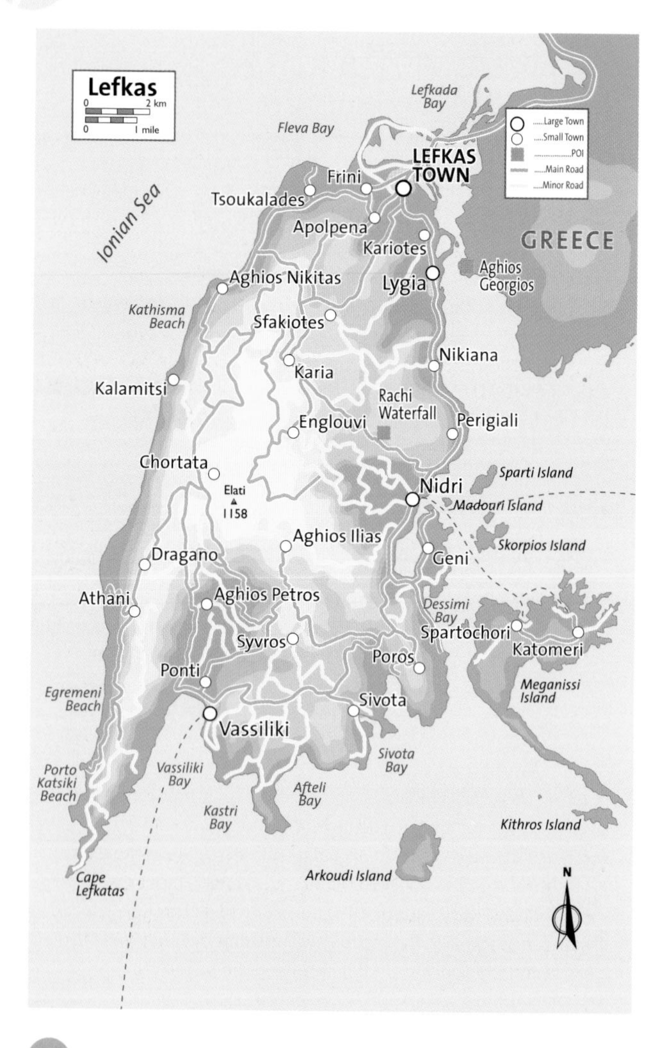
Lefkas
0
2 km
0
1 mile
Large Town
Small Town
POI
Main Road
Minor Road
Lefkada Bay
Fleva Bay
Ionian Sea
LEFKAS TOWN
Frini
Tsoukalades
Apolpena
Kariotes
GREECE
Aghios Nikitas
Lygia
Aghios Georgios
Kathisma Beach
Sfakiotes
Nikiana
Karia
Kalamitsi
Rachi Waterfall
Englouvi
Perigiali
Chortata
Elati
1158
Sparti Island
Nidri
Madouri Island
Aghios Ilias
Skorpios Island
Dragano
Geni
Athani
Aghios Petros
Dessimi Bay
Spartochori
Katomeri
Syvros
Poros
Ponti
Meganissi Island
Egremeni Beach
Sivota
Vassiliki
Sivota Bay
Porto Katsiki Beach
Vassiliki Bay
Afteli Bay
Kastri Bay
Kithros Island
Cape Lefkatas
Arkoudi Island
N

Lefkas Town

Lefkas Town (also known as Lefkada) sits at the northernmost tip of Lefkas island, separated from mainland Greece by a lagoon known as the Ichthiotrofrío – literally, 'the fish pond' – where herons and pelicans wade in search of food. Though flattened by an earthquake in 1953, the town has a great deal of charm because of its narrow traffic-free alleys. As a precaution against further earthquakes, many houses were built with timber upper storeys, to help spread the load.

The main street, **Odhos Dörpfeld** (also known as Idanou Mela), is named after the late 19th-century archaeologist who spent much of his private income on excavations in the fruitless attempt to find the palace of Odysseus, hero of Homer's *Odyssey*. In and around this street you will find most of the town's popular bars and restaurants, which bustle with life in the summer.

BEACHES

Just west of the town, the 4-km (2½-mile)-long sand and shingle beach of **Vira** (**Gyra**) is big enough to accommodate all visitors. Beyond the windmill is a second beach, named **Aghios Ioannis Antzousis** after the nearby Crusader chapel. Further south are the two sandy beaches of **Kathisma** and **Pefkoulia**.

IS LEFKAS AN ISLAND?

Lefkas was attached to mainland Greece by a narrow strip of land until the 6th century BC, when a canal was dug through the isthmus, turning what had been part of the mainland into an island. Today Lefkas is connected to the mainland by a bridge, which opens every hour, on the hour, to let boats through. You can walk across the causeway to explore the ruins of Santa Maura castle on the mainland, originally built in the 14th century.

THINGS TO SEE & DO

Archaeological Museum

An excellent small museum with informative new displays, showcasing the best finds by archaeologist-hero Wilhelm Dörpfeld in ancient Leukas town, halfway between Lefkas Town and Lygia.
ⓐ 1 Aggeou Sikelianou, Cultural Centre ⓣ 26450 21635 ⓛ 08.30–15.00, closed Mon ⓘ Admission charge

Churches

Lefkas has several fine frescoes painted by members of the Ionian School of artists, who were influenced by Italian Renaissance painting, and whose work is often more naturalistic than that of their contemporaries. Their work is to be found in private chapels, with

A curious earthquake-proof tower in Lefkas Town

erratic opening hours (try to get in just after the daily service). The best examples are in the church of **Aghios Dhimitrios** (ⓐ Zabelion), the churches of the **Pantokrator** and **Theotokou** (ⓐ Both on Dörpfeld) and the church of **Aghios Minas** (ⓐ On the junction of Ioannou Mela and Merarchias).

Faneromeni Monastery

This pretty timber-built monastery, with a museum and small chapel full of colourful stained glass, was originally built in 1634. Hanging in the courtyard is a log that was beaten to call the monks to prayer during World War II, when the ringing of bells was banned by the German occupiers, fearful that the monks would use the bells to transmit coded messages.

ⓐ 4 km (2½ miles) outside Lefkas ⓛ 09.00–13.00, 18.00–20.00

Folklore Museum

Island life is illustrated through a small collection of festive embroidered costumes, furniture and domestic items. Also on display are photographs of the town before the destructive 1953 earthquake, and models of some of the prehistoric settlements uncovered by the archaeologist Dörpfeld in the 19th century.

ⓐ Theodorou Stratou, opposite OTE phone office ⓣ 26450 22473
ⓛ 10.00–13.00, 19.00–22.00 ⓘ Admission charge

Phonograph Museum

This small museum just behind the Bazaar giftshop, south of Lefkas's main square, contains a zany selection of early gramophones, cameras,

SHOPPING

The best place for souvenir shopping is the pedestrian precinct in **Odhos Dörpfeld**, off the main square. You will find plenty of small shops selling ceramics, pottery and local food.

photographs and jewellery boxes dating from between 1850 and 1920. The museum sells CDs of Greek music too.
Ⓐ Kalkanou Ⓣ 26450 21088 Ⓛ 10.00–14.00, 18.00–24.00

Windsurfing

Windsurf Club Milos (Ⓣ 26450 21332) can teach you the tricks of the trade, or else simply rent their gear on Aghios Ioannis Antzousis beach.

TAKING A BREAK

Café Agora £ Popular coffee and sweet shop which also serves *ouzo*, ice cream and sandwiches. Trendy atmosphere and popular with locals – great views of everyday Greek life. Ⓐ 101 Dörpfeld Ⓣ 26450 23580 Ⓛ 08.00–23.00

Café Karfakis £ Lovely old-fashioned bar decorated with old photographs which maintains the tradition of serving little morsels of food – *mezedes* – with your drinks. Ⓐ 125 Dörpfeld Ⓣ 26450 26730 Ⓛ 08.00–15.00, 19.00–23.00

Eftychia £ A small taverna hidden just off the busy main street. You can point out which ready-made vegetable, salad and pasta dishes you want, and order additional freshly grilled meats or fish. Has a very local, untouristy atmosphere. Ⓐ 3 Stampogli, near Sikelianou Ⓣ 26450 24811 Ⓛ 08.00–24.00

Enjo £ Snacks, ice cream and waffles on the busy stretch between the harbour and the main square. Ⓐ 10 Dörpfeld Ⓣ 69367 78271 Ⓛ 08.30–03.00

Gustoso ££ Popular with Greeks and holidaying Italians, this restaurant specialises in pasta, pizzas and a range of ice creams and cocktails. Also provides a takeaway service. Ⓐ Aggelou Sikelianou Ⓣ 26450 24603 Ⓛ 11.00–01.00

AFTER DARK

Restaurants

Ey Zin £ A wonderful, inexpensive taverna serving 'soul food' just off the main drag. Great salads, spaghetti with mussels, and Lefkas specialities such as wine pork with peppers. ⓐ 8 Filarmonikis ⓛ 18.00–00.30

Lighthouse ££ Delightful garden and a good choice of local dishes. ⓐ 14 Filarmonikis ⓣ 26450 25117 ⓛ 17.00–23.00

Romantika ££ Large restaurant just off the main street with a huge menu and daily Greek dancing and folk song shows. ⓐ 11 Mitroupoleos ⓣ 26450 22235 ⓛ 11.00–02.00

Voglia di Pizza £££ Upmarket restaurant on the waterfront serving Greek and Italian dishes in a cool and sophisticated ambience. ⓐ Aggelou Sikelianou ⓣ 26450 26461 ⓛ 17.00–23.30

Nightlife

The liveliest nightspots are in and around the harbour end of Dörpfeld, most with bars and café tables spilling out on to the street. The best place for open-air music and dancing is Club Milos on Yira beach. During the week-long International Folklore Festival in late August, buskers entertain the crowds throughout the city centre.

Casbah Café ££ The funkiest place on the square, Casbah serves breakfast, salads, sandwiches by day and makes great cocktails later on at night. On the speakers: rock and Latino. ⓐ Main square ⓣ 26450 25486 ⓛ 08.30–02.00

Karma ££ Lefkas Town's trendiest café-bar, perfectly located on the bustling waterfront. By day there's coffee and snacks, while at night the music is turned up and cocktails are the drink of choice. ⓐ Corner of Dörpfeld and Aggelou Sikelianou ⓣ 26450 23623 ⓛ 07.00–05.00

Lygia

Lygia (pronounced 'Lig-yah'), just 5 km (3 miles) south of Lefkas Town, has an attractive harbour and looks across to the ancient fortress of Aghios Georgios (St George) on the mainland. The pace of life is slow and relaxed with just a couple of hotels, supermarkets and restaurants strung unpretentiously along the 2-km (1¼-mile) stretch of resort.

To the south of the fishing port is a small shingly beach backed by shady trees and within walking distance of some very attractive waterside fish tavernas, where you can watch fishermen bring in their catch. Further north is the hamlet of Kariotes, noted for the weekly Wednesday clothing market beside the village square. For nightlife, it is better to head to the clubs and bars in Lefkas Town, or to neighbouring Nidri if you want to book a boat trip.

BEACHES

Further south there are some fine beaches and wonderful views of the mainland at **Nikiana** and at **Perigiali**.

THINGS TO SEE & DO

Boat trips

Most organised boat trips depart from nearby Nidri (see page 22) and are therefore just a short bus or car drive away. Ask around at the harbour for occasional trips departing from Lygia, or rent a boat from Trident boats (☎ 69366 49984) and plan your own day trip.

Horse riding

At the Swedish-run Arami's Farm (☎ 26450 26190), halfway between Lefkas Town and Lygia, you can learn horse-riding basics or join guided tours of the island.

TAKING A BREAK

Bill's Snack Bar £ This simple restaurant set beneath a fig tree and grape vines serves English breakfast, chicken, chops, pitta bread and salads. ⓐ Lygia main road ⓣ 26450 71556 ⓛ 11.00–01.00

Seagull £ Lygia's breeziest and most modern café, with 40 types of crêpes, sandwiches and ice cream. Sit on the terrace and enjoy the sea view while the kids play board and PC games inside. ⓐ Harbourfront ⓣ 69775 97894 ⓛ 10.00–02.00

Green Stop ££ Welcoming restaurant with waterside views. Specialises in pizzas, pasta and traditional Greek meals; try the tasty grilled meat options. ⓐ Lygia harbourfront ⓣ 26450 72140 ⓛ 08.00–03.00

To Limani ££ Also known as Maxis, this good-value waterside fish taverna has friendly service. ⓐ Lygia harbourfront ⓣ 69473 27289 ⓛ 11.00–24.00

O Xouras ££ This fish taverna, named after the owner, offers a good range of freshly caught fish. You can eat in or out at tables right beside the waterfront. ⓐ Lygia harbourfront ⓣ 26450 71312 ⓛ 11.00–02.00

O Yiannis ££ Good-value grilled fish, lobster and other seafood, although there are meat and salad dishes too. Overlooking the sea. ⓐ Lygia harbourfront ⓣ 26450 71407 ⓛ 10.00–02.00

Nidri

Nidri lies on the east coast and enjoys lovely views of the wooded islets of Sparti, Madouri, Skorpidi and Skorpios. Although Nidri is Lefkas's busiest and biggest resort town, with a good choice of shops, it is still pretty laid-back and retains the feel of traditional Greece.

BEACHES

Nidri's two beaches are narrow and shingly and can get crowded during July and August. For a quieter, sandy beach, head south to **Dessimi**.

THINGS TO SEE & DO

Boat trips

From the quay in Nidri, you can take a wide variety of boat trips to the delightful offshore islands. Nearby islands include privately owned Madouri, uninhabited Sparti and Skorpios, and Meganissi, with its sea cave at Papanikolis. A day trip on the MS *Christina* sailing boat (t 06450 31805) passes the islands of Kastos and Kalamos. The *Ikaros* (t 26450 92134) is a

The shingle beach at Nidri

comfy cruise ship that does a daily seven islands tour, stopping off at Kefalonia, Ithanaka, Meganissi and Madouri, among others.

Diving

The **Dream Divers** team (t 69458 51475 w www.iddivers.com) offers everything from trial dives to full scuba-diving courses.

Rachi Waterfall

Take a 90-minute stroll from Nidri to the hamlet of Rachi for a cooling dip in a natural pool below these pretty waterfalls. The route is signposted from the centre of Nidri. Take water to drink as there is only one taverna on the way.

Watersports

Waterskiing, inflatable flyfish, bananas, ringos, parasailing and more fun can be had at **Nidri Watersports** (t 26450 92084 w www.watersportsinlefkada.gr) on the main beach.

TAKING A BREAK

Café di Paris £–££ Not only will you find wonderful ice cream at this pleasant café, but also a fine English breakfast, waffles, pizza and cocktails. Free Wi-Fi Internet. a Waterfront t 26450 92235 o 08.00–04.00

The Barrel ££ A bright restaurant with a spotless open kitchen overlooking the northern part of the harbour. Serves Greek and local Lefkada cuisine. a Waterfront t 26450 92906 w www.thebarrel.gr

La Dolce Vita ££ First-class Italian food cooked by Italian chef. a Nidri waterfront t 26450 93206 o 18.00–02.00

George's Place ££ Greek taverna run by lively local called George. Try the *gyros* (sliced pork kebabs with salad, chips and tzatziki rolled in pitta bread). a Nidri main road t 26450 92689 o 09.00–23.00

Vassiliki

Vassiliki is 16 km (10 miles) southwest of Nidri and lies in a huge bay sheltered by mountains. Although the pebble beach may not be ideal for swimming, for windsurfing it is regarded as one of the best in Europe. The bay is alive with brightly coloured sails skimming across the water and there are plenty of places offering tuition and equipment if you come unprepared.

The breezes, which make Vassiliki so perfect for windsurfing, are just right for beginners in the morning, grow stronger as the day goes on, and then die down by dusk. The narrow streets of the tiny village bustle with visitors, and the lively nightlife draws young people from all over the island.

BEACHES

The pebble beach runs along the entire bay. The best beach is at **Ponti** at the northern side of Vassiliki Bay, where a watersports centre offers windsurfing and waterskiing.

Vassiliki is great for windsurfing and boat trips

THINGS TO SEE & DO

Boat trips

Water-taxis leave from Vassiliki harbour to the white cliffs of Cape Lefkatas (see page 30) and the pretty white beach of Agiofili. The waters at Agiofili are crystal clear and perfect for snorkelling. Take your own food and drink as there are no facilities, although sunbeds and parasols are available for hire. There are ferries to Kefalonia throughout the day.

Diving

Halfway along the bay, the **Nautilus Diving Club** (t 69361 81775) offers snorkelling and scuba-diving trips, from trial dives to complete courses.

Land activities

Try horse riding or rent bicycles, mountain bikes or a car to explore the olive groves and flower fields around **Syvros**, one of the bigger villages to the north. Ask your tour rep, hotel or local tourist office for details.

TAKING A BREAK

Dolphin Restaurant £ Traditional cuisine such as fish soup, swordfish and grills served on outside tables decked in green and white tablecloths. a Waterfront t 26450 31430 b 11.00–24.00

Ionio Café £ A pleasant café in the middle of the waterfront, serving delicious fresh crêpes and waffles, ice cream and coffee. Also has Internet access. a Waterfront t 26450 31965 b 07.30–04.00

WINDSURFING

Vassiliki beach attracts windsurfers from across Europe and beyond. It is rated among the top ten windsurfing places in the world, with perfect conditions for racing, slalom and freestyle stunts.

JoMil £ Run by two convivial brothers, this café has the best fresh fruit juices and coldest beers in town. Try the fruit salad or some home-made treats such as baklava and chocolate cake. ⓐ Waterfront ⓣ 26450 31396 ⓛ 08.00–01.00

Yannis Grill House £ Snacks and fast food served with a smile. ⓐ Waterfront ⓣ 26450 31446 ⓛ 11.00–02.00

Restaurants and cafés line the harbour walls in Vassiliki

Mythos £–££ Popular and friendly taverna serving great breakfasts, Greek and international lunch and dinner, and cocktails at night; it also has a pool for lounging around. ⓐ Ponti road, opposite campsite ⓣ 26450 31414 ⓛ 08.00–02.00

Alexander ££ Fresh fish and seafood, served in both Greek and Italian styles, with good harbour views. ⓐ Waterfront ⓣ 26450 31355 ⓛ 09.00–23.00

Pirate Restaurant ££ A friendly and popular choice for pirate-wannabes. Its shaded terrace is good for people-watching in the evenings. ⓐ Port road ⓣ 26450 31837 ⓛ 11.00–24.00

Stelios ££ Baked vegetables, lamb and peppered steaks are just some of the Mediterranean and Greek dishes on offer here. Located at the western end of the harbour. ⓐ Waterfront ⓣ 26450 31566 ⓛ 11.00–02.00

Miramare ££–£££ Sit on the largest terrace on the seafront, at the eastern end of the harbour, to sample the excellent spaghetti and traditional moussaka. Miramare's fish arrives in the afternoon and is always very fresh. ⓐ Waterfront ⓣ 26450 31909 ⓛ 09.00–01.00

AFTER DARK

Abraxa's Tunnel Run by an old hippy who is happy to talk philosophy, the Tunnel is a small but lively music bar playing oldies and Greek rock to a mostly local audience. ⓐ Port road ⓣ 69728 75333 ⓛ 20.30–05.00

155 Vassiliki's coolest lounge bar has chilled music and a minimal white interior with arty photos. Late at night, DJs spin music in the soundproofed bar. ⓐ Port road ⓛ 09.30–14.00, 19.00–04.00

Vass Bar A colourfully lit bar with loud house music and balcony overlooking the harbour. ⓐ Port road ⓣ 26450 31427 ⓛ 09.00–05.00

Lefkas excursions

Lygia and Nidri both make an excellent base for exploring the island. Inland, you can visit ancient churches with time-worn frescoes and mountain villages, where the womenfolk create delicate lace and embroidery following centuries-old traditions. The sandy beaches of the west and south coasts, tucked into coves between the wild limestone cliffs of the western shores, are ideal for every kind of watersports activity.

LACE VILLAGES

Karia

Karia is the main production centre for the lace and embroidery that is sold all over the island, and there is an excellent selection here of handmade products, as well as carpets and other textiles. Even if you do not want to shop, this mountain village is worth visiting for its excellent folklore museum, the **Museum Maria Koutsochero** (09.00–21.00 Admission charge), run by a long-established family of lacemakers. Housed in a typical peasant's home, the furnishings, equipment and utensils give you a good idea of a village way of life that only just survives.

The tree-shaded main square has a number of bars and restaurants, and a tea shop where you can have English tea and toasted sandwiches. In August, a re-enactment of a Greek wedding party takes place in the square; a bride and groom parade through the village on horseback, wine flows, and there is plenty of merriment. Karia is 8 km (5 miles) south of Lefkas Town.

Englouvi

Close to Karia is Englouvi, another lace village and the highest settlement on Lefkas (730 m/2400 ft above sea level). Set in a green valley on the slopes of Mount Elati (1158 m/3800 ft), the village is famous for its green lentils, prized all over Greece, and during August free lentils and home-baked bread are offered to visitors.

Porto Katsiki's glorious beach

THE WESTERN & SOUTHERN COASTS

Aghios Nikitas

With its jumble of timber-clad buildings spilling down the bottom of a gorge to a pebble beach, Aghios Nikitas is easily the most photogenic and picturesque village on Lefkas. Flowers and vines hang from balconies along the narrow street, and provide shade for the terraces of old tavernas. You can swim here in the refreshingly cool and crystal-clear waters below the village or take a sea-taxi to the long, sandy beach at nearby Mylos.

Kalamitsi

Kalamitsi is reached via steep roads with many a hairpin bend. The views from this typical mountain village are best appreciated over a drink or lunch in one of the traditional tavernas, and the shops are well stocked with souvenirs, such as locally made embroidery.

Cape Lefkatas

Also known as Cape Doukato, the gleaming white rock at the southwesternmost tip of the island is the original Lovers' Leap. It was from here that Sappho, the ancient Greek poetess, threw herself into the waves. Although she was better known as a lesbian (the term derives from Lesbos, the island of Sappho's birth), it was her unrequited love for a man – the handsome Phaeon – that drove her to her suicide. Today a lighthouse tops the 60-m (197-ft) high rock, from which people still hurl themselves, though nowadays they are usually strapped to a hang-glider.

Sivota

Sivota, a quiet fishing village on the south coast between Vassiliki and Nidri with a string of fish tavernas, is a safe anchorage for yachts. You can enjoy pleasant strolls around the bay watching fishermen unload their catch and spreading out their nets to dry. But for the best views, make your way to the top of the cliff where a taverna perched on the cliffside overlooks the bay.

BEACHES

Egremeni

Reached by 260 steep steps from the road that runs across the top of Cape Lefkatas, Egremeni has a fine, sandy beach. It is one of Lefkas's most beautiful beaches, but it does tend to become crowded by mid-morning as visitors arrive by boat from Vassiliki. The beach shelves steeply and there can be occasional currents, so beware when swimming. Egremeni is at the southwestern tip of the island.

Kathisma

Kathisma is a sandy beach that lies a few minutes' drive south of Aghios Nikitas. The road to the beach is good, and there is plenty of parking available. From here, a winding road continues southwards to Cape Lefkatas, remarkable for its coastal and mountain scenery. The road dips into valleys, climbs into the mountains and swings down into bays with sandy beaches.

Porto Katsiki

A rock slide in 1998 caused the beach to be cut in two, but the clear blue waters and white shingle beach, framed by white cliffs, still make Porto Katsiki one of the best and most famous beaches on Lefkas. Most people arrive by boat from Vassiliki, but you can get there by descending 60 steps from the main road. Mobile food stalls sell drinks and snacks, which tend to be expensive, so it is better to take your own with you. There is a good road leading to the beach and car parking. It is popular with tourists and can get busy during the summer.

Kefalonia
0
10 km
0
5 miles
N
Ionian Sea
Adipata
Fiskardo
Frikes
Stavros
Kioni
Xalikeri
Evreti
Anogi
Ithaka
Assos
Vathy
Komitata
Myrtos Beach
Perachori
Divarata
Atheras
Agia Efimia
Kardakata
Kefalonia
Antisamos Beach
Kalata
Kourkoumelata
Melissani
Lake & Cave
Sami
Mount Evmorfia
Drogarati Caves
Grizata
Lixouri
Lepeda
ARGOSTOLI
Aghios Gerasimou
Monastery
Aghios
Nikolaos
Chavriata
Lassi
Ammoudia Beach
St George's
Castle
Mount Ainos
Poros
Akrotiri Bay
Lakythra
Metaxata
Kefalonia
Keramies
Svoronata
Pessada
Ruins of the
Temple of Apollo
Porto
Skala
Kourkoumelata
Lourdata
Pastra
Katelios
Skala
City
Large Town
Small Town
POI
Main Road
Minor Road
Airport

Argostoli

Tragedy struck Argostoli in 1953 when the graceful island capital was all but destroyed by a major earthquake. Today all traces of the disaster have disappeared and the town has been rebuilt using some traditional materials. Many attractive older buildings remain, including the gracious mansions along the palm-lined streets to the north of the main square, Plateia Vallianou.

Plateia Vallianou is the social centre of the town, and the location of the evening *volta*, when everyone comes out to stroll, chat with their friends and enjoy the cooler air. Equally good for a stroll is the lively waterfront, with its balconied shops and tavernas. From here, there are views across the Koutavos lagoon to the wooded slopes of Mount Evmorfia. The tourist office is at the northern end of the seafront promenade, and ferries depart from here every hour for Lixouri (see page 44).

At the southern end of the harbour is the 800-m (2625-ft) Drapanos Bridge, built in 1813 by the Swiss-born British governor of the island, Colonel Philippe de Bosset. Local people initially opposed the causeway, fearing it would bring undesirable elements into the town from the villages on the other side of the lagoon!

BEACHES

The best beaches are at Lassi (see page 39) but you can cool off at the new lido to the north of the town and use the bar and café.
Admission charge

THINGS TO SEE & DO

Anny Cinema

An outdoor garden cinema showing current major releases in English, usually in two showings. During early season, the late show is best as the screen can be indistinct in the light evening.
16 Xarokopoy 26710 25880 June–Aug only Admission charge

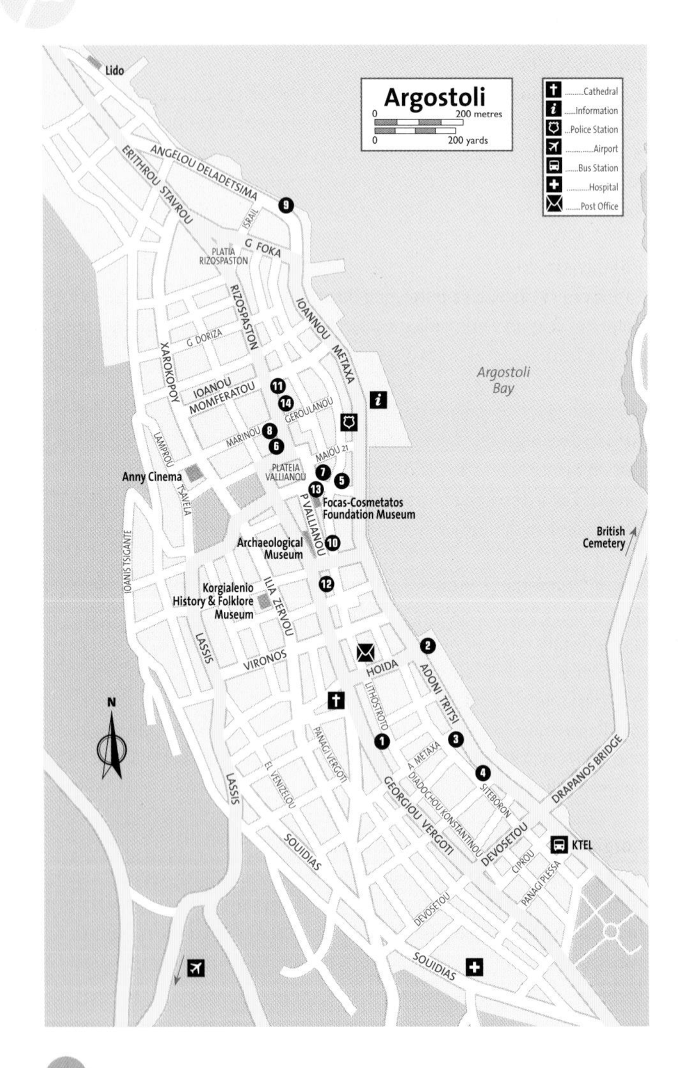
Argostoli
0 200 metres
0 200 yards
Cathedral
Information
Police Station
Airport
Bus Station
Hospital
Post Office
Lido
ANGELOU DELADETSIMA
ERITHROU STAVROU
ISRAIL
G FOKA
PLATIA RIZOSPASTON
RIZOSPASTON
IOANNOU METAXA
G DORIZA
XAROKOPOY
IOANOU MOMFERATOU
GEROULANOU
MARINOU
LAMPROU
MAIOU 21
PLATEIA VALLIANOU
Anny Cinema
TSAVELA
Focas-Cosmetatos Foundation Museum
P VALLIANOU
Archaeological Museum
IOANIS TSIGANTE
Korgialenio History & Folklore Museum
ILIA ZERVOU
LASSIS
VIRONOS
HOIDA
ADONI TRITSI
LITHOSTROTO
PANAGI VERGOTI
A METAXA
DIADOCHOU KONSTANTINOU
GEORGIOU VERGOTI
SITEBORON
EL VENIZELOU
LASSIS
SOUIDIAS
DEVOSETOU
CIPROU
PANAGI PLESSA
KTEL
DEVOSETOU
SOUIDIAS
DRAPANOS BRIDGE
British Cemetery
Argostoli Bay
N

Archaeological Museum

Everything you need to know about ancient Kefalonia packed into two rooms, including 3000-year-old pottery from the Mycenaean period and a statue of Pan, the goat-like god of shepherds and wild things.
ⓐ Georgiou Vergoti ⓣ 26710 28300 Ⓛ Tues–Sun 08.30–15.00
ⓘ Admission charge

Boat excursions

Take a cruise on a glass-bottomed boat from the harbour to spot dolphins, visit ancient sunken shipwrecks, and photograph marine life. Details from Port Authority kiosk on waterfront.
ⓣ 26710 22224

British Cemetery

Dating back to the 1820s and the British Protectorate, though not a War Graves' Commission cemetery, it's worth a visit.
ⓐ Fifty metres on right, after crossing Drapanos Bridge from Argostoli

Focas-Cosmetatos Foundation Museum

This quirky museum houses English lithographs of the local countryside and a wealth of other historical material. The Foundation is linked to the beautifully landscaped Cephalonia Botanica gardens with Mediterranean plants, located on the edge of town.
ⓐ 1, P Vallianou ⓣ 26710 26595 Ⓛ 09.30–13.00, 19.00–22.00 Mon–Sat (closed Mon eve). Garden open 08.30–14.30 Tues–Sat ⓘ Admission charge (ticket includes garden)

Korgialenio History & Folklore Museum

A well-presented account of island culture and history, shown through a series of reconstructed rooms, from the cave-like poverty of a peasant farmer's dwelling to the richly furnished rooms of a wealthy mansion.
ⓐ Ilia Zervou ⓣ 26710 28835 Ⓛ Tues–Sat 09.00–14.00 ⓘ Admission charge

TAKING A BREAK

Many good restaurants, bars and tavernas are found around Argostoli's main square and its side streets, or along the harbourfront road called Ioannou Metaxa.

Bell Tower Café £ ❶ Housed in an elegant tower, this unique café is run by mentally and physically handicapped people. Try the home-made lemonade and don't miss the exhibition of pre-earthquake photos and the view from the top. ⓐ 52B Lithostroto ⓣ 26710 24456 ⓛ 09.00–21.00

Elios £ ❷ Friendly, family-run taverna-café with traditional village-style dishes and *mezedes*. Bouzouki music evenings; popular with both locals and visitors. ⓐ 62a Tritsi ⓣ 26710 23650 ⓛ 09.00–23.00

Tsilikos £ ❸ Long-established *souvláki* and grill house. Try the chicken or pork *gyros* (kebabs). Large portions ideal for hungry eaters. ⓐ Adoni Tritsi ⓣ 26710 22304 ⓛ 10.00–24.00

Kalafatis ££ ❹ Old family recipes prepared in a traditional charcoal oven. Enjoy the sea views near the Drapanos Bridge. ⓐ Adoni Tritsi ⓣ 26710 22627

Kohenoor ££ ❺ The only authentic curries on Kefalonia. All your favourites, spiced to your liking on request. Children's menu. ⓐ 2 Lavragka, off Plateia Vallianou ⓣ 26710 26789 ⓛ 18.30–24.00

Il Palazzino ££ ❻ The largest restaurant on the square is part of the Ionian Plaza hotel and serves a wide range of Greek, Italian and international dishes. ⓐ Plateia Vallianou ⓣ 26710 25580 ⓛ 19.00–01.00

Paparazzi ££ ❼ Enjoy fine Italian cuisine on a quiet terrace just off the main square. ⓐ 2 Lavragka ⓣ 26710 22631

Captain's Table £££ ❽ Perhaps Argostoli's most popular eatery, with upmarket dishes and prices. Try fresh fish or lobster. ⓐ 3 Rizospaston, also on the harbourfront, corner of Maiou 21 ⓣ 26710 23896 ◷ 11.00–24.00

Kiani Akti £££ ❾ Family-run restaurant specialising in *mezedes*, good wines and *ouzo*. The restaurant occupies its own jetty to the north of town. ⓐ Ioannou Metaxa ⓣ 26710 26680 ◷ 12.00–23.00

AFTER DARK

Bass Club ❿ Large, late-night Greek-style clubbing, party theme nights and visiting DJs in high season. International music every night except for Greek night on Thursdays. ⓐ Rokou Vergoti ⓣ 26710 25020 ⓦ www.bassclub.gr

Bodega ⓫ A rocking beer bar with a modern two-storey interior, the Ionians' fanciest toilets, regular jazz concerts, and no less than 115 beers on the menu, of which 7 are on tap. Snacks include ice cream, cakes and great fruit salads. ⓐ 14 Rizospaston ⓣ 26710 22022 ◷ 08.00–04.00

Metropolis Café ⓬ By day a pleasant café, by night it becomes the prime nightspot along the shopping street, with a classy first-floor terrace and fountain. ⓐ 4 Lithostrato ⓣ 26710 29069 ◷ 07.00–03.00

Café Platanos ⓭ The most pleasant café on the main square, with comfy indoor and outdoor seating and photos of old Argostoli on the walls. By night it turns into a jam-packed bar with regular Greek rock nights. ⓐ Plateia Vallianou ◷ 08.00–03.00

De Stijl ⓮ The coolest cocktail bar along the nightlife stretch with a stylish interior and outside seating along the Philharmonic building. DJs and dancing on weekend nights. ⓐ 15 Rizospaston ⓣ 26710 23446 ◷ 18.00–04.00

Kalamia beach is overlooked by white cliffs

Lassi

Lassi is the name of the peninsula that separates the sheltered Koutavos lagoon, to the east, from the larger Gulf of Argostoli to the west. Since the arrival of tourism on Kefalonia, resort developments have spread along the west coast of the peninsula, from its northern tip, all the way down to the airport, about 11 km (7 miles) south.

Based in Lassi, you are never far from the island's capital, which is a 30-minute hike over the hill, or a 90-minute romantic stroll along the coastal road known as 'lovers' walk'. Lassi is ideally situated to make the most of the white-sand beaches of western Kefalonia (see map on page 32) and the enchanting village settlements south of Lakythra, set in olive groves and fruit orchards.

BEACHES

Kalamia

Close to the centre of Lassi, Kalamia is set in a picturesque bay, with white cliffs backing a grey sand and shingle beach. Sunloungers and umbrellas are for hire and there is a small bar.

ⓐ 2 km (1¼ miles) north of Lassi centre on the Fanari/Agostoli scenic road

Makris Yialos

This long stretch of golden sand is very popular but big enough not to get impossibly crowded. It's perfect for families, with sheltered warm water, watersports equipment and beach furniture for hire; there's also a large café at the southern end and others above, overlooking the beach.

ⓐ 800 m (880 yds) south of Lassi centre

Paliostafida

Just in front of the Mediterranee Hotel, this beach has grey sand and clear sea; sunbeds and umbrellas are available for hire.

ⓐ Lassi centre

Platis Yialos

Golden sands and facilities that include showers and changing rooms.
ⓐ 1 km (1/2 mile) south of Lassi centre

Tourkopodaro

This peninsula of white beach has umbrellas and sunbeds mainly used by the White Rocks Hotel guests, but you can swim from neighbouring Platis Yialos and enjoy the views. The White Rocks Hotel is 1.5 km (1 mile) from Lassi centre.

TAKING A BREAK

Aquarius Café Bar ££ Pleasant family-oriented café-bar that serves snacks, ice creams and the best cocktails in the resort, plus TV sports' coverage and a wide selection of music. ⓐ Central Lassi, main street ⓣ 26710 23556 ⓛ 09.00–02.00

AFTER DARK

International £ Traditional local grill dishes, pasta and delicious pizzas, with occasional musicians. ⓐ Lassi main road ⓣ 26710 41388 ⓛ 11.00–23.00

Mystic Gusto ££ A fine Greek taverna with a vine-covered terrace, pleasant service and a children's corner. ⓐ Main road ⓣ 26710 25970 ⓛ 08.00–01.00

The Olive Press ££ Flower-bedecked taverna with an old olive press outside. Welcoming atmosphere and open all day for breakfast, lunch and dinner. Live music nightly. ⓐ Minies, airport road ⓣ 69780 52263 ⓛ 11.00–24.00

Phaedra ££ For romantic open-air dining, this restaurant has Greek music, a children's menu and a fine selection of local wines which you

can buy from the barrel to take home. Italian, Greek and English menu. Try the special Greek omelette. Major credit cards taken. ⓐ Lassi main road ⓣ 26710 26631 ⓛ 10.00–23.00

San Lorenzo ££ Attractively set around a courtyard, San Lorenzo serves traditional Kefalonian and Italian dishes. Child-friendly menu and facilities. ⓐ Lassi centre, near to Makris Yialos ⓣ 26710 25660 ⓛ 11.00–23.00

Sirtaki ££ Lively Greek taverna with traditional décor serving home-made local dishes, fresh fish and choice of bottled or barrelled wine. ⓐ Lassi main road ⓣ 26710 23852 ⓛ 12.00–24.00

Sto Psito ££ Popular with locals and visitors alike, this friendly taverna serves up local specialities and barrel wine. ⓐ Fanari road ⓣ 26710 25306 ⓛ 17.00–23.00

Chinese Dragon £££ Authentic Chinese restaurant with magnificent views of the sunset, and children's playground. ⓐ Fanari road ⓣ 26710 22005 ⓛ 19.00–24.00

La Gondola £££ Italian restaurant with cosy ambience. Well-stocked bar and excellent range of Italian and Greek dishes. Ideal venue for a special night out. ⓐ Lassi main road ⓣ 26710 25522 ⓛ 11.00–23.00

SHOPPING

You can do all your shopping in Lassi's main road. Try **Veronica's** (ⓣ 26710 22191) for exquisite handmade jewellery, **Vagelati Supermarket** (ⓣ 26710 25590) for fresh fruit and vegetables, liquor and local wines, and **Lassi Supermarket** for a good range of provisions, holiday essentials, newspapers and magazines, etc.

Monte Nero £££ Try traditional *mezedes* and the huge variety of fresh fish; international dishes too. Local barrel wine and extensive wine list of over 90 well-known wines from all over Greece. Relaxing atmosphere, fine service and beautifully furnished. ⓐ Lassi main road ⓣ 26710 22646 ◷ 18.30–01.30

EXCURSIONS

Corelli's Kefalonia Tour

Following in the footsteps of Captain Corelli, the central figure in *Captain Corelli's Mandolin*, this tour starts at the Italian War Memorial on the Lassi peninsula and continues to the small village of Kourkoumelata, rebuilt after the 1953 earthquake. You can see examples of pre-earthquake houses at Svoronata and visit Metaxata where Lord Byron stayed for four months. To the north is the 13th-century monastery of Aghios Andreas (St Andrew) and an ecclesiastical museum, and behind it, the now ruined fortress of Aghios Georgios (St George), with fine views across the south coast.

Mount Ainos

The island's highest peak at 1628 m (5340 ft), covered in native fir trees once famous throughout Greece and used in building the palace at Knossos on Crete, is now a national park, grazed by wild horses. A road goes part way up; thereafter walk to the summit along a rough track. ⓐ 20 km (12 miles) east of Lassi

HOLIDAY READING

If you are looking for a good book to read while lazing on the beach, try *Captain Corelli's Mandolin* by Louis de Bernières. This tells the story of the Italian invasion of the island in World War II and the events that led to the mass execution of 5,000 Italian soldiers, known as the Kefalonia martyrs, on Hitler's direct orders. Gloomy as this sounds, the novel is full of lively humour and presents an authentic portrait of Greek island life.

Sea kayaking

To see more of the beautiful Kefalonian coast, join a sea kayak excursion. **Sea Kayaking Kefalonia** (Lygia, south of Lassi 69340 10400, www.monte-nero-activities.com) has safe, guided trips for beginners and pros around Kefalonia and Lefkas.

Wine from Kefalonia

Kefalonia produces some of the best white wine to be drunk anywhere in Greece. Several wineries can be visited, so you can see wine being produced and try some varieties. The large **Robola Producers' Co-operative** in Omala, beside Ayia Gerassimos church, 3 km (2 miles) south of Lassi (26710 86301 www.robola.gr 07.00–15.00 Mon–Fri) welcomes visitors, as does the more exclusive **Gentilini Winery** (Minies, main road 26710 41618 www.gentilini.gr 10.30–14.30, 18.00–20.30 Mon–Sat (July–Aug); evenings only June & Sept).

Makris Yialos is Lassi's most popular beach

Lixouri

Lixouri sits on the western side of the Gulf of Argostoli, looking across to the island's capital, which is only 30 minutes away by ferry (services half-hourly in high season from 07.30 to 01.00). Despite being the island's second-largest town, Lixouri is quiet and friendly, little touched by tourism and a good place to enjoy Grecian island life.

The statue of Andreas Laskaratos (1811–1901), situated by the ferry port, commemorates a poet who was also a noted wit. When the local priest excommunicated him for his irreverence, saying that his body would never rot unless he repented, Laskaratos rushed home to get his children's ragged clothes and hole-filled shoes, asking the priest to excommunicate them too. Beyond the ferry port is the main square with its shaded cafés. One of the few buildings to survive the earthquake of 1953 is now the town's **Museum**, which has a small collection of religious icons (Ⓐ Western side of the main road towards Hotel Palatino Ⓣ 26710 91325 Ⓛ 08.30–13.30 Tues–Sun Ⓘ Admission charge).

BEACHES

Akrotiri

A small bay with a sweep of golden sand; no facilities but peaceful.
Ⓐ 10.5 km (6½ miles) south of Lixouri

Ammoudia (also known as Xi)

Red sand contrasts with chalk-white cliffs at this beach, which has a hotel and two tavernas. Sunbeds and umbrellas available for hire.
Ⓐ 8 km (5 miles) south of Lixouri

Lepeda

Sandstone rocks, carved into weird sculptures by the wind, shelter this beach and provide a safe natural pool for children to bathe in. Sunbeds and parasols can be hired, and there's a taverna nearby.
Ⓐ 2 km (1¼ miles) south of Lixouri

The waterfront at Lixouri

Lixouri

Lixouri's nearest beach is a narrow strip of sand just south of the town centre, which is popular with families.

TAKING A BREAK

Dionysos Musi Café £ Good selection of coffees, teas, cocktails, snacks, sweets, ice creams, etc. ⓐ Main square ⓣ 26710 94208 ⓛ 09.00–03.00

Nostimon Inmar £ An arty café on the pedestrianised street behind the waterfront. Sip coffee in a relaxed atmosphere, listen to jazz or play chess with a friend while the hours pass by. ⓐ G Lampraki ⓣ 26710 93680 ⓛ 09.00–04.00

Oasis £ Cosy and comfortable pizzeria serving Greek and Italian fare, English breakfasts, ice creams, sweets and drinks. ⓐ Main square ⓣ 26710 93384 ⓛ 10.00–02.00

AFTER DARK

Canta Napoli £ Traditional Greek and Italian goodies, including delicious pies, served in a lively ambience. Good wines. Families welcome. ⓐ Main square ⓣ 26710 92238 ⓛ 10.00–01.00

Acrogiali £–££ This simple Greek taverna serves some delicious local specialities; the lamb dishes are well worth trying. The taverna is run by a woman from New Jersey in the US, who fell in love with Kefalonia and never left. ⓐ Waterfront ⓣ 26710 92613 ⓛ 12.00–01.00

Novita Restaurant ££ Spacious seating in the upstairs terrace overlooking the waterfront. Good wholesome dinners; the house speciality is fresh fish. Music bar. ⓐ Andrea Laskaratou ⓣ 26710 94251 ⓛ 10.00–24.00

Sami

Sami has the island's largest harbour and lies 22 km (14 miles) northeast of Argostoli along the bay of the same name. According to Homer, ancient Sami stood outside the town to the north and the ruins are still visible on the hills next to the harbour. These days Kefalonia's main ferry port has a pleasant taverna-lined seafront and a fine pebble beach just north of the port.

TAKING A BREAK

Captain Jimmy £–££ Simply the best ice cream, pastries and cakes in town, eaten inside or on the waterfront terrace. ⓐ Main square ⓣ 26740 22059 ⓛ 08.00–02.00

Dolphins ££ Popular family-run establishment. Excellent local dishes of grills and fresh fish. Features local musicians and singers on Wednesdays and Saturdays. ⓐ Waterfront ⓣ 26740 22008 ⓛ 09.00–03.00

Faros ££ Great home cooking in this friendly, family-run taverna which is the oldest in town. Try anything from the big grill. ⓐ Waterfront ⓣ 26740 23041 ⓛ 10.00–24.00

Karavomilos ££ Right on the seafront with a view of the duck-filled Karavomilos Lake. Try Kefalonian meat pie, lobster, *kalamari* or *pastitsio*. ⓐ Karavomilos ⓣ 26740 22216 ⓛ 11.00–24.00

Nea Sami ££ One of the first coffee shops in Sami, dating back to 1870. Excellent cakes and popular with the locals. Try a *metrio* (medium-sweet Greek coffee). ⓐ Waterfront ⓣ 26740 22024 ⓛ 08.30–01.00

Captain Corelli's ££–£££ A fancy but pricey café cashing in on the Corelli book and film craze. Ice creams, waffles and snacks are all available. ⓐ Waterfront ⓣ 26740 22128 ⓛ 07.30–01.00

Skala

Skala lies 31 km (19 miles) southeast of Argostoli. Blessed with a long beach and low sand dunes, it is developing into a major tourist resort. The original village sat on a hill inland but, following the 1953 earthquake, was moved to its present site beside the sea. Modern Skala is laid-back and easy-going with fairly low-key nightlife, but the area is perfect for snorkelling and there are Roman ruins to explore. The 2-km (1¼-mile) sand-and-shingle beach, fringed by pink and white oleander, is big enough never to be seriously overcrowded. Sunbeds and umbrellas can be hired by the day and there are plenty of watersports.

THINGS TO SEE & DO

Adventure sports

It's easy to explore nature with **Kefalonia's Activities** (t 26710 83311), which arranges regular walking, mountain biking, camping and diving trips. You can combine a night camping on a small island with a canoe trip.

Boat trips

Most organised boat trips leave from Lassi, involving a trip there first, but **Captain Kostis** (t 69362 17283) does daily cruises directly from Skala to nearby beaches, ports and sights.

AFTER DARK

Restaurants

Pikiona ££ Upmarket swimming pool complex which includes a Greek restaurant and bar. Try the hydromassage and workouts in a garden setting. Music by DJs until late. a Beach road t 26710 83410 w www.pikiona.gr 09.30–01.00

Sunrise ££ The last taverna overlooking the quiet western end of the beach is well worth a visit. The owners, Victor and Fotoni, serve up

Intricate mosaic from a Roman villa in Skala

fantastic fish and grilled meat dishes. Ⓐ Beach road Ⓣ 26710 83125 Ⓦ www.skala-sunrise.gr Ⓛ 08.00–24.00

Manor House ££–£££ Kefalonian specialities and wines are served at this very elegant restaurant in the village centre. Great garden views from the balcony terrace. Next to Sally's. Ⓐ Main road, behind the church Ⓣ 26710 83182 Ⓛ 11.00–02.00

The Old Village ££–£££ An elegant restaurant and cocktail bar decorated with mementos of the old Skala village from before the earthquake. Try the chicken stuffed with tomatoes. Ⓐ Main road Ⓣ 26710 83513 Ⓛ 08.30–24.00

The Pines Restaurant ££–£££ Corner location in pretty flower-bedecked restaurant giving good views of the street. Try the Greek or Italian specialities and barrel wine. Down on the beach, there's 'The Pines Too'. Ⓐ Main road Ⓣ 26710 83216 Ⓛ 08.00–24.00

Fiskardo

Fiskardo escaped serious damage during the 1953 earthquake and is the island's prettiest village. Venetian-style houses cluster around the bay, and excellent dining opportunities are on offer.

BEACHES

Two pebble beaches are a short distance from the village. Emblisi beach is a ten-minute walk north. A 20-minute walk to the south brings you to Foki beach, set in a beautiful cove with olive trees, cypresses and a good taverna (t 69447 57032 ⌚ 12.00–18.30).

THINGS TO SEE & DO

Boat trips

The environmental club in the museum (**FNEC** t 26740 41081 w www.fnec.gr) organises boating, dolphin-spotting, snorkelling and scuba-diving trips, combined with a guided tour of the museum so that you can make the most of the experience. Several boats like the *Nautilus* (t 26740 41440) do daily trips to Ithaka and the small islands near Lefkas, departing from Fiskardo around 10.00.

Nautical & Environmental Museum

Contains an exhibition about the biology and ecology of Fiskardo and the area. Also on display are parts of a Bristol Beaufighter bomber.
a Old school, near the main car park t 26740 41081 ⌚ 10.00–18.00 Mon–Fri, 10.00–14.00 Sun, closed Sat

TAKING A BREAK

Anemoessa ££ A good place in which to relax after sailing into port and for trying fish specialities you won't find at home – the swordfish is delicious. a Waterfront t 26740 41267 ⌚ 11.30–24.00

Fiskardo's peaceful Foki beach

Apanzio ££ Near the ferry jetty, you can try fresh fish, grilled meat, pasta and vegetarian dishes at this breezy waterside restaurant. Waterfront 26740 41260 11.00–02.00

Greco ££ A tiny bistro with waterfront seating and a very friendly owner who has travelled the world and likes to chat to his guests. Lounge music, free Wi-Fi, drinks and snacks. Waterfront 26740 41380 08.30–02.30

Lord Falcon £££ Fiskardo's only ethnic food is served at this great little Thai restaurant. Popular with visiting yachties, you can have your green curry as spicy as you like. Fiskardo village 26740 41072 17.00–01.00

Kefalonia excursions

BEACHES, VILLAGES & RUINS

Aghios Gerasimou Monastery

This building was founded by the island's patron saint, whose mummified remains are kept in a beautiful silver casket on view during his festival days. Magnificent examples of Ionian icon/fresco paintings. Please dress modestly. Close to the Siroke Robola Co-op Winery, Valsamata

Antisamos Beach

This white-pebbled, crescent-shaped beach with the most verdant of mountain backdrops provides a unique opportunity to get away from it all. The snorkelling is superb. Sunbeds and sun umbrellas for hire.
It is a good idea to take your own food as there is only one mobile food stall and taverna on the beach. 4 km (2½ miles) east of Sami

Assos

The unspoiled village of Assos clings to the island's western coast. The ruined Venetian fortress (1595) can be reached by footpaths from the small harbour. The protective walls once sheltered the villagers of Assos from the ravages of pirates. 22 km (14 miles) north of Lixouri

Drogarati Caves

The huge Drogarati Caves drip with stalactites and, with their excellent acoustics, are occasionally used for concerts. Note that you have to descend 120 steps to reach the entrance and that you will need to dress warmly as it is chilly in the caves. 3.5 km (2 miles) southwest of Sami
08.00–19.00

Ithaka

One of the most popular trips from Sami is the 30-minute ferry to neighbouring Ithaka. Numerous temples and ruins on the island are linked with Odysseus, including the capital, Vathy, with its Venetian fortresses and the stalactite-hung Cave of the Nymphs, 2 km (1¼ miles) to the west.

Melissani Lake & Cave

The Melissani Cave was used as a temple in pre-Christian times by worshippers of the god Pan. Visitors explore the cave by boat, lit from above by a hole in the cave roof. ⓐ 4 km (2½ miles) northwest of Sami ⓒ 08.00–19.30

Myrtos Beach

Spectacular Myrtos (Mirtos) is everybody's idea of the perfect beach, with its half-moon of silver shingle sliding into the shallows of an azure-blue sea. Sunbeds and umbrellas for hire. ⓐ 18 km (11 miles) north of Lixouri

Neighbouring islands

Lefkas (see page 14) and Zakynthos (see page 54) are both within easy reach of Kefalonia, with daily ferry services from Fiskardo and Pessada.

Poros

Poros has direct ferry links to Kilini on the mainland. Warm turquoise waters and delightful fish tavernas ⓐ 13 km (8 miles) north of Skala

Ruins of the Temple of Apollo

These 7th-century BC ruins were discovered next to the tiny church of Aghios Georgios. The waters here are ideal for snorkelling. ⓐ Porto Skala, 2 km (1¼ miles) north of Skala

St George's Castle

Once guarding the Venetian-era capital of the island, later destroyed by an earthquake, the impressive hilltop ruins of St George's Castle (Kastro), which are visible from Argostoli, make for a good stop on the way east to Skala. ⓐ Peratata village, 5 km (3 miles) south of Argostoli ⓒ 08.30–09.00 Tues–Sun

Wineries

South Kefalonia produces some fine wines, and several wineries are open for visitors to see how their wine is made (see page 43).

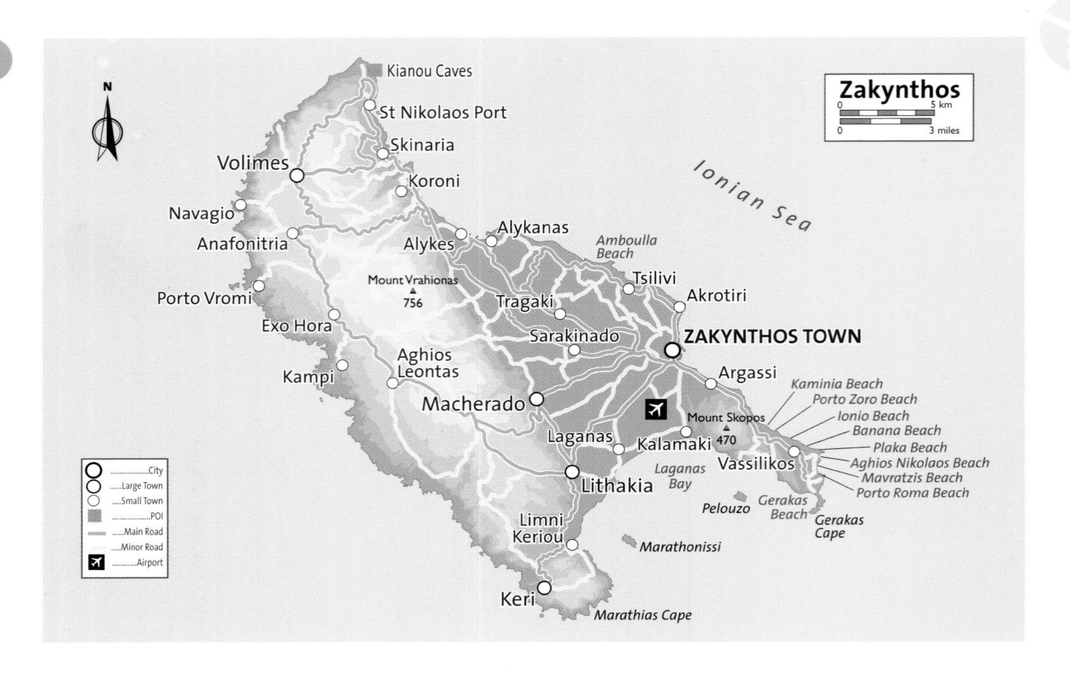

Zakynthos
0 5 km
0 3 miles
N
Kianou Caves
St Nikolaos Port
Skinaria
Volimes
Koroni
Navagio
Anafonitria
Alykes
Alykanas
Ionian Sea
Amboulla Beach
Mount Vrahionas 756
Tsilivi
Akrotiri
Porto Vromi
Tragaki
Exo Hora
Sarakinado
ZAKYNTHOS TOWN
Aghios Leontas
Kampi
Argassi
Macherado
Kaminia Beach
Porto Zoro Beach
Mount Skopos 470
Ionio Beach
Banana Beach
Laganas
Kalamaki
Plaka Beach
Vassilikos
Aghios Nikolaos Beach
Laganas Bay
Mavratzis Beach
Lithakia
Porto Roma Beach
Pelouzo
Gerakas Beach
Gerakas Cape
Limni Keriou
Marathonissi
Keri
Marathias Cape
City
Large Town
Small Town
POI
Main Road
Minor Road
Airport

Zakynthos Town

You would not know that the capital of Zakynthos (also known as Zante) had been destroyed by an earthquake in 1953, so well has the town been rebuilt in a style that tries to recapture the former elegance of a town once known as the 'Flower of the Levant'. Ruled by Venice for over 300 years, the streets of Zakynthos are a refreshing blend of Grecian and Venetian styles, with traditional arcades running round the two main squares and along Alexandrou Roma, the main shopping street, and providing welcome shade from the sun.

Zakynthos's busy harbour is alive with craft of all kinds: fishing boats unloading their catch, inter-island ferries, sleek yachts and luxurious cruise ships. To the south of the harbour stands the church of Aghios Dionysios (St Dennis), one of the few buildings to survive the earthquake, with a tall campanile (bell tower) modelled on the one in St Mark's Square in Venice. Some local people attribute the survival of the church to the protection of St Dennis, whose mummified body lies inside in a silver coffin; others to the reinforced concrete structure of the building.

On the craggy hilltop above the town there are the ruins of the ancient Venetian kastro, or fortress, where townspeople sheltered from piratical raids. More like a miniature town than a castle, the kastro offers superb views from its walls. Passing through gateways carved with the lion of St Mark, symbol of Venice, you can explore the remains of old chapels, warehouses and barrack buildings (08.00–19.30 Admission charge).

AGHIOS DIONYSIOS

Aghios Dionysios (St Dennis) is the island's patron saint and his feast day is celebrated on 24 August. On this day, the saint is given a new pair of slippers, because it is believed that he wears out the old ones wandering around the island doing good deeds.

THINGS TO SEE & DO

Boat trips

A variety of travel agents along the Zakynthos Town waterfront offer day trips around Zakynthos and neighbouring islands. **Zante Voyage** (ⓐ 12 Agiou Dionysiou ⓣ 26950 25360 ⓦ www.zantevoyage.gr) is an excellent, helpful travel agency in Zakynthos Town that can arrange car and motorbike rental, horse riding and local excursions. Popular destinations for stops, swimming and barbecues are Shipwreck (Navagio) Bay, Makrys Gialos beach and the Blue Caves.

Byzantine Museum

Photographs and scale models show what Zakynthos Town looked like before the 1953 earthquake. There is also an outstanding

The campanile of Aghios Dionysios towers above the harbour

SHOPPING
The two main shopping streets in Zakynthos Town are Alexandrou Roma and Maiou, leading into the main square of Agiou Markou, with its tree-shaded cafés. Tourist shops sell ceramic turtles and the local specialities, *mandoláto* (white honey-flavoured nougat with almonds) and *pustéli* (bars made of honey and sesame seeds).

collection of frescoes and religious paintings from churches all over the island.
ⓐ Plateia Solomou ⓣ 26950 42714 ⓒ 08.00–15.00 Tues–Sun
ⓘ Admission charge

Nautical Museum
Contains exhibits of the nautical history of Greece – the only museum in Greece to portray the country's nautical history from 1700 BC to the present day. See the display of ships that took part in the Greek Revolution of 1821.
ⓐ Fillikon near Strani Hill ⓣ 26950 28249
ⓒ 09.30–14.30, 18.30–22.30 ⓘ Admission charge

Tourist Train
Several times a day, a tourist train (ⓣ 69443 76963) departs from the Zakynthos Town waterfront for the 15-minute trip to Argassi. There are also regular guided tours of the town.

TAKING A BREAK

Deals £ Modern café along the shopping street with shady seating in the adjacent alley. Friendly service, good coffee and light snacks.
ⓐ 16 Alexandrou Roma ⓣ 26950 45900 ⓒ 07.30–01.00

San Marco £ The best terrace on the main square belongs to the relaxed San Marco café. While away the time people-watching or borrow one of the chessboards. Snacks include ice cream and sandwiches.
ⓐ Plateia Solomou ⓣ 26950 45701 ⓛ 09.30–03.00

Porto £–££ Bar snacks on the pier. Good place to watch the inter-island ferries while sipping an *ouzo*. ⓣ 26950 29190 ⓛ 08.00–02.00

AFTER DARK

Restaurants

Arekia ££ Considered by many to be the island's best traditional taverna and often crowded with locals. Local folk song performances from 22.00.
ⓐ Dionissiou Roma ⓣ 26950 26346 ⓛ 10.00–01.00

Zakynthos Town's elegant buildings

O Kilos ££ At this simple outdoor restaurant opposite the cathedral (Kilos means garden) you can try local specialities such as Zakynthos-style rabbit, washed down with *ouzo*. ⓐ 64 Dionissios ⓣ 26950 48583 ◷ 09.00–23.00

Squero ££ A popular grill house on the corner of the bustling main square. On the menu are grilled meat and fish, vegetarian options and children's dishes. ⓐ Plateia Ag Markou ⓣ 26950 24000 ◷ 08.00–02.00

Arestis Piano Bar/Restaurant £££ Overlooking the sea, this taverna/restaurant serves international fare and is tastefully furnished. Dress up and enjoy the views. ⓐ Akrotiri ⓣ 26950 27379 ◷ 09.00–23.00

Panorama £££ Upmarket venue with sweeping views over Zakynthos in the nearby hamlet of Bokhali. Serves local dishes as well as international food. Booking advised. ⓐ Bokhali ⓣ 26950 28862 ◷ 11.00–23.00

Venetziana International £££ Enjoy the cool night air while sampling Venetziana's Italian, Greek and international cuisine. ⓐ Plateia Ag Markou ⓣ 26950 23722 ◷ 09.00–02.00

Nightlife

Café Chanté A wonderful, hidden café with a flagstone floor and wafting silk curtains separating the cosy tables. Come for coffee, salads, snacks and cocktails. ⓐ Frangopoulou ⓣ 69991 72731 ◷ 19.00–03.00

Casino Café A large, swanky café overlooking the square from a raised terrace. The food menu is limited to snacks and desserts, but the cocktail list is impressive. ⓐ 4 Plateia Solomou ⓣ 26950 29107 ◷ 09.00–02.00

Mille Labra Halfway down the waterfront, this bar is the best of a clutch of nightlife options. By day there's coffee, by night the small space fills with a party crowd dancing to DJ music. ⓐ 24 Lombardou ⓣ 26950 24409 ◷ 08.00–02.00

Argassi

Argassi is a family resort with a fine beach on the doorstep, 1 km (1/2 mile) in length and offering a wide variety of watersports. The town provides plenty of nightlife opportunities and is only a short distance from the capital, Zakynthos Town (see page 55).

Argassi is an excellent base for exploring Mount Skopos, the highest point on the island rising to 470 m (1540 ft) and a good place to look for wild orchids and rare butterflies. The name of this mountain means 'Look-out' and you will understand why if you travel to the summit: the views take in the whole of the island and the nearby Peloponnese, as well as the Bay of Navarino in between, site of a major naval battle in 1827.

TAKING A BREAK

Remezzo Beach Bar £ An all-in-one spot for eating and drinking (from breakfast through to dinner, and beyond), popular Remezzo's has loungers with waiter service and a swimming pool for cooling off. ⓐ On the beach ⓛ 08.00–24.00

Capriccio ££ Excellent Greek food is served with flair at this romantic restaurant with good views over the town and waterfront. ⓐ Waterfront ⓣ 26950 42818 ⓛ 09.00–24.00

Carrissimo ££ Traditional Greek and international food, including the local Zakynthian beef stew. Friendly staff and shaded terrace. ⓐ Main road ⓣ 26950 45669 ⓛ 10.00–24.00

Granada Taverna ££ This friendly, family-run restaurant specialises in Greek dishes, but also offers good pastas and pizzas. ⓐ By the main road ⓣ 26950 43512 ⓛ 10.00–24.00

Green Frog ££ A popular British-run restaurant in the centre of town, serving everything from breakfast to dinner and cocktails. There's a lovely garden at the back and games to keep the kids happy. ⓐ Main road ⓣ 26950 22596 ⓛ 08.30–01.00

Papillon Ristorante ££ Up on the main road, Papillon does hearty Italian fare, as well as steaks and tasty desserts. ⓐ Main road ⓣ 26950 43720 ⓛ 09.00–24.00

Stars ££ Popular taverna, on the main street but away from the throng. ⓐ Argassi coast road, opposite the bank ⓣ 26950 42875 ⓛ 10.00–01.00

Venetziana ££ Try rabbit Zakynthos-style at this Greek restaurant, set back from the main road. Live Greek music at night. ⓐ Five-minute walk inland from the Magic Mushroom bar ⓣ 26950 26230 ⓛ 17.00–02.00

AFTER DARK

Avalon Bar This friendly, revved-up bar just back from the waterfront is known for its potent cocktails and international crowd. ⓐ Near the waterfront ⓣ 26950 42787 ⓛ 17.00–03.00

Beer Academy This sports bar has pool tables and big-screen TVs for football, and serves beers, cocktails and coffees. ⓐ Near the Diana Palace Hotel ⓣ 26950 43903 ⓦ www.thebeeracademy.com ⓛ 09.00–03.00

Legends A bar with theme nights, entertainment and large screens to watch all the latest sports action. Serves food as well. ⓐ Main road ⓣ 26950 27624 ⓦ www.legends-bar.com ⓛ 08.00–04.00

Magic Mushroom Right in the centre of the resort, this is a popular bar at which to meet up or end up. ⓐ Main road ⓛ 10.00–04.00

Red Lion With a dozen draught beers and more than 50 bottled beers, cocktails and a wide range of snacks, the Red Lion is a popular sports bar. ⓐ Main road ⓣ 26950 43815 ⓛ 10.00–03.00

Vassilikos

Vassilikos is situated on the southeastern tip of Zakynthos, on the peninsula formed by the mountain range that separates this resort from those at Kalamaki and Argassi. Arguably the prettiest part of the island, the peninsula offers a wealth of coves and beaches backed by lush pines.

Just one road links the small villages that make up the Vassilikos peninsula, along which traditional tavernas and restaurants are strung. Car or motorbike hire is essential to explore this part of the island.

BEACHES

Aghios Nikolaos

Watersports facilities – and a bar perched on top of a rocky outcrop in the middle of the beach – attract visitors to this sandy spot, 3 km (2 miles) south of Vassilikos. There is also a large, modern hotel, with swimming pool and restaurants, open to non-residents.

Banana Beach

Nobody seems to know how this beach got its name, but Banana Beach is a popular spot just south of Vassilikos, with bars and watersports facilities.

ECOTOURISM

The National Marine Park in Laganas Bay is a protected area due to the rare loggerhead turtles that lay their eggs on the beaches. **Nature World Travel** (Gerakas beach, Vassilikos ⓣ 26950 36029 ⓦ www.natureworldtravel.com) organises special eco-day trips from Zakynthos port and Vassilikos on the *Argo* catamaran boat, taking in Sekania nesting beach, Keri and Marathonissi island, with time for swimming and turtle spotting. There's a trained guide on board who will explain all about sea turtles and the marine park. Departure from Zakynthos port at 09.00, Aghios Nikolaos beach 09.45, Mavratzis beach 10.00, and Porto Roma beach 10.15.

Loggerhead turtles are quite rare

Gerakas

Some say that this beach is the best in the Ionian Islands; it certainly has all the ingredients: golden sand, warm shallow waters and shelter from the wind provided by sandy cliffs. There are two tavernas and a snack bar but no watersports, because of the breeding turtles.

Porto Roma

Small, sheltered cove with a sand and pebble beach, plus bar and taverna, 5 km (3 miles) south of Vassilikos.

TAKING A BREAK

Coffee House £ Drop in for coffee, *ouzo* or cocktails at this friendly coffee house; try the *tsikoudia*, a clear, schnapps-like drink. Vassilikos village 26950 35333 08.30–23.00

Mais Café £ Simple alfresco meals. No menu, but ask for the butter beans in tomato sauce, tzatziki and special meatballs. ⓐ Vassilikos main road ⓣ 26950 35232 ⓛ 08.30–22.00

Lithies £–££ Meaning 'stones', Lithies serves a good range of local dishes (village-style chicken, Zakynthian beef stew) plus fresh fish and wine from the farm's vineyards. ⓐ Vassilikos village ⓣ 26950 35290 ⓦ www.lithieshouses.gr ⓛ 10.00–23.00

Agnadi ££ Terraced taverna with panoramic views over the coast. Greek cooking and a relaxing, family-run atmosphere. ⓐ Xirokastello, Vassilikos ⓣ 26950 35337 ⓛ 09.00–23.00

Dioscuri ££ Family cooking in a pleasant garden setting. Try the *mezedes* of grilled pepper, aubergines, aubergine salad and taramasalata. ⓐ Vassilikos village ⓣ 26950 35162 ⓛ 09.00–23.00

Galini ££ Family-run taverna, with fresh fish, grills and plenty of parking. You can stroll in the nearby forest, and there is a play area for the children. ⓐ Near Gerakas beach, south of Vassilikos village ⓣ 26950 35231 ⓛ 09.00–23.00

O Gallos ££ Excellent French/Greek restaurant with a singing and bouzouki-playing owner. ⓐ Vassilikos village ⓣ 26950 35460 ⓛ 09.00–24.00

Giovanni's ££ A lively traditional taverna serving rabbit and delicious kokinisto beef stew. ⓐ Vassilikos village ⓣ 26950 35471 ⓛ 12.00–23.00

Kostas Brothers ££ A flower-filled garden and terrace. Regular performances of traditional songs to guitar and mandolin accompaniment. Try the delicious pork roast, stuffed with garlic and herbs. ⓐ Vassilikos village ⓣ 26950 35347 ⓛ 09.30–23.00

Beach umbrellas provide welcome shade at Plaka beach

To Steki ££ A Greek taverna serving traditional meals on a beautiful bougainvillea-clad terrace. Friendly service. Ⓐ Xirokastello, Vassilikos Ⓣ 26950 35205 Ⓛ 09.00–23.00

Triodi ££ Some unusual offerings of *mezedes* and grills at this Greek taverna on the way to Gerakas beach. Ⓐ Gerakas–Vassilikos Road Ⓣ 26950 35215 Ⓛ 11.00–23.00

AFTER DARK

Calypso A snack and cocktail bar with sports on large screens, entertainment, Internet access and food ranging from English breakfasts to Greek dinners. Ⓐ Porto Roma road Ⓛ 09.00–02.00

Loggos Enjoy generous cocktails in the tree-shaded garden. Air-conditioned dance floor and regular themed parties. Ⓐ Vassilikos village Ⓣ 26950 35296 Ⓛ 12.00–01.00

Kalamaki

Kalamaki is a relaxed family resort whose beach is an extension of that at Laganas, offering the same clean, golden sands and clear waters.

The beach is five minutes from the resort centre and is relatively quiet, due to nesting loggerhead turtles. There are showers available, and pedalos, canoes, umbrellas and sunbeds for hire. Because of the nesting turtles, visitors to the beach are asked not to stick umbrellas in the sand in the marked nesting zones, or to dig up the turtle eggs. Use of the beach is banned during the hours of darkness.

THINGS TO SEE & DO

Horse riding

Kids can spend a morning pony riding in the countryside. Details from the **Riding Centre**, Kalamaki. ⓣ 69445 20519

Mini Golf

There's fun for all ages to be had at the 18-hole **Kalamaki Mini Golf**. Golf balls and clubs are provided, and refreshments and snacks are available. ⓐ In the centre of Kalamaki resort ⓛ 10.00–01.00 (April–Oct)

TAKING A BREAK

Buon Amici ££ Popular Italian restaurant with indoor, air-conditioned seating area, and terrace. Excellent range of Greek and Italian wines. ⓐ Main road ⓣ 26950 22915 ⓛ 12.00–23.00

Maharaja ££ Spicy Indian curries and smooth kormas. Also serves a range of Chinese dishes. ⓐ Main road ⓣ 26950 24715 ⓛ 17.00–23.00

Michaelos ££ A well-known, family-run taverna with a friendly atmosphere; the chef is happy to cook special dishes on request. ⓐ Main road ⓣ 26950 48080 ⓛ 09.00–23.00

Kalamaki beach

Pelouzo ££ Guests at this taverna attached to the Crystal Beach Hotel can enjoy varied English and Greek food as well as make use of the swimming pool overlooking the seafront. Try the daily specials from bean soup to steak Diane. ⓐ Kalamaki beach ⓣ 26950 53039 ⓗ 09.00–23.00

Zepo's Taverna ££ Excellent Greek dishes served with a sea view. One of the few beachside restaurants in Kalamaki. ⓐ Kalamaki beach ⓣ 26950 27698 ⓗ 10.00–23.00

AFTER DARK

Fire Club Kalamaki's hottest bar, with bartenders slinging bottles around before pouring you a cocktail. ⓐ Main road ⓣ 26950 24328 ⓗ 12.00–03.00

Laganas

Laganas has possibly the finest beach on Zakynthos, a 4-km (2½-mile) sweep of golden sand, gently shelving into a jewel-like sea as warm as bath water. This bay is also the nesting area for around 80 per cent of the Mediterranean's population of the loggerhead turtle, and conservation measures now in place ensure that there is no danger to the turtles from speedboats and jet-skis. This makes for a relatively quiet life on the beach, though the nightlife is the liveliest on Zakynthos.

BEACHES

Laganas Bay

The ban on watersports imposed to protect the loggerhead turtles means that this is a quiet family beach, perfect for children because of the warm shallow water and fine sand, with plenty of room for everyone. The stretches of beach nearest the resort can be busy, but you do not have to walk far to find a less crowded spot. Sunloungers for hire.

Laganas beach with Cameo Island in the distance

THINGS TO SEE & DO

Go-Karting

Near the airport runway, Laganas Go-Kart (t 69442 82826) has the best track on the island. (For non-racers, there's mini-golf too.)

TAKING A BREAK

Jacket Potato Place £ Just what you need for a cheap and filling lunch: jacket potatoes with scores of different fillings to choose from. a Main road t 26950 51195 ⏲ 10.00–01.00

Mama's Place £ Snacks and meals served in simple settings. Good for *souvláki*, *gyros* and lamb kebabs. a Main road t 26950 52729 ⏲ 10.00–01.00

Akropolis ££ Beautiful countryside setting, surrounded by olive groves. a Pandokratoras t 26950 51168 ⏲ 10.00–23.00

Giorgio's ££ Lively restaurant run by Greek–Canadian family, with American and oriental dishes on the extensive menu, including stir-fries, steaks and ribs. a Kalamaki road t 26950 52255 ⏲ 09.00–23.00

EGGS IN THE SAND

The breeding season for the shy loggerhead turtle coincides with the main holiday season. During July and August, the females come ashore to lay their eggs about 50 cm (20 inches) below the surface. The eggs are insulated by the warm sand, and the baby turtles hatch some eight weeks later, crawling towards the bright moon-lit sea. **Archelon**, an organisation set up to save the loggerhead turtles, takes volunteers to work on the island (t 21052 31342 w www.archelon.gr).

Horizon ££ Aptly named for the wide views across the bay, come here for the breakfasts or the Greek and international dishes. ⓐ Laganas beach ⓣ 26950 52791 ⓛ 08.00–23.00

Tasos Taverna ££ Excellent Greek fare, including fresh fish specialities, is served at this classy place right on the beach. ⓐ Laganas beach ⓣ 26950 53265 ⓦ www.tasostaverna.gr ⓛ 09.00–01.00

AFTER DARK

Restaurants

Panos & Kostas ££ An authentic Greek taverna and grill in the heart of the resort. Home cooking, grilled meat and fresh fish. ⓐ Kalamaki road ⓣ 26950 52931 ⓛ 08.30–24.00

Paradise ££ This elegant but reasonably priced townhouse restaurant specialises in traditional lamb and chicken dishes, as well as fresh fish such as sea bass. ⓐ Main road, near Paradise Apartments ⓣ 26950 52516 ⓛ 09.00–23.00

Popolaros Tavern ££ Excellent meat, cheese and vegetable *mezedes* (Greek appetisers) and hearty portions of rabbit or beef *stifado* (stew) are among many local specialities here. Live Greek music is also on offer. ⓐ Main Laganas–Keri road ⓣ 26950 45461 ⓛ 09.00–24.00

ZAKYNTHOS

The name of Zakynthos is said to derive from the wild hyacinths that still grow on this lush, green island, which the Venetians nicknamed the 'Flower of the Levant'. The luxuriant landscape is planted with orange and olive groves, almond orchards and vineyards, producing tiny sweet grapes for drying and turning into succulent raisins.

Taj Mahal ££ As a change from Greek food, why not try this Indian restaurant specialising in chicken tikka massala, seafood and meat curries, and the house special biryani? ⓐ Kalamaki road ⓣ 26950 51783 ⓛ 18.00–24.00 ⓦ www.tajmahal-rest.gr

I Fratelli ££–£££ Serves Mediterranean and local cuisine with bay view seating. Try the *midia saganaki* (mussels in sauce) starter followed by steak. ⓐ Beach road ⓣ 26950 51178 ⓦ www.ifratelli.gr ⓛ 09.00–23.00

Sarakina £££ Live Greek music and dancing makes a meal here more of an occasion. Set in the hills, 10 km (7 miles) from the centre with free transport available, and with good views over the nearby mansion ruins and the hills. ⓐ Sarakina Mansions ⓣ 26950 51606 ⓛ 12.00–24.00

Nightlife

The hub of Laganas's nightlife is the main road just inland from the beach, with a wide choice of bars and clubs and lots of party people. The music is mainly hip hop, R&B and dance.

Bad Boys A popular R&B and hip-hop club near the beach. A fun place to party till the sun comes up. ⓐ Main road, waterfront ⓣ 69457 03550 ⓛ 22.00–05.00

Cameo Island Club Reached by a wooden bridge from the beach, this small island houses two Caribbean-style bars. Also open during the day and serves snacks. ⓐ Laganas beach ⓣ 26950 23398 ⓛ 09.00–03.00

Cocktails & Dreams Trendy young nightspot based on the bar from the film *Cocktail* and serving a mix of 50 cocktails with dance music. ⓐ Main road ⓛ 17.00–04.00

Medousa Fringed by illuminated palm trees, this large bar and club on the main strip is great for a night of mindless partying to house and dance music. ⓐ Main road ⓦ www.medousabar.gr

Keri

At the end of Laganas Bay, Limni Keriou has a small harbour with several restaurants and a sandy beach. The small village of Keri, a ten-minute drive into the mountains from the bay, escaped the worst effects of the 1953 earthquake, and some fine old Venetian-style buildings have survived. A path from the village goes to the lighthouse at the southernmost tip of the island, with cliffs eroded into strange shapes by the wind and waves.

THINGS TO SEE & DO

Boat trips

Several boat owners offer taxi services to isolated beaches nearby, and there are daily dolphin- and turtle-spotting trips.

Beach sports at Keri

Diving

The **Diving Center Turtle Beach** (ⓐ Limni Keriou ⓣ 26950 49424 ⓦ www.diving-center-turtle-beach.com) has everything from beginners' trial dives to full PADI courses.

TAKING A BREAK

Kafeneion Panaiotis Liveris £ This charmingly local grocery store and café on Keri village's main square is as authentically Greek as it gets, offering simple but delicious salads, snacks and drinks. ⓐ Keri village ⓛ 09.00–17.00

Anemomylos ££ Panoramic views over the coast and pine-clad countryside can be had from this modern restaurant serving Greek and English food, snacks and drinks. ⓐ Located beside the windmill on the Limni Keriou–Keri road ⓣ 26950 52650 ⓛ 09.00–01.00

To Keri ££ A breezy terrace overlooking the beach, with breakfast, good pastas and grilled meat. ⓐ Limni Keriou waterfront ⓣ 26950 43756 ⓛ 10.00–23.30

Spitiko ££ Traditional Greek food including grilled fish and oven-baked dishes, served on a cool, green terrace with sea view. ⓐ Limni Keriou waterfront ⓣ 26950 49198 ⓛ 12.00–24.00

To Fanari ££–£££ Delicious home-made wine and home-style cooking in a romantic cliff-top location with dazzling views of the rocks and waves far below. The Greek flag in the car park is the largest in the world! ⓐ 2 km (1 mile) beyond Keri village ⓣ 26950 43384 ⓛ 10.00–22.00 ⓦ www.liveris.gr

La Bruschetta £££ A beautiful Italian restaurant in a cypress forest overlooking the bay. Enjoy top-quality pasta dishes or the best pizzas on Zakynthos. ⓐ Limni Keriou–Keri road ⓣ 26950 28128 ⓛ 18.45–01.00

The golden sands of Tsilivi

Tsilivi

Tsilivi (pronounced 'Sill-ivi') is just 5 km (3 miles) north of Zakynthos Town and 9 km (5½ miles) from the airport, on the northeast coast of Zakynthos. The long, safe beach of soft sand and clear waters has plenty to offer in the way of watersports. The huge bay attracts windsurfers and waterskiers and offers activities such as paragliding and pedalo and ringo rides. In spite of plenty of shops, bars, tavernas and restaurants, Tsilivi's traditional charm still attracts young couples and families. To the west of Tsilivi are more uncrowded beaches via short access roads through delightful orchards and vineyards.

BEACHES

Amboulla

Golden sands, quiet and with just a few tavernas 1 km (½ mile) to the west of Bouka beach. A dive centre on the beach provides watersports.

Bouka

Small, clean and sandy beach with shallow water; rarely crowded.

Planos

Planos, an extension of Tsilivi, has several tavernas and shops. Umbrellas and parasols can be hired by the day.

SHOPPING

The **Tom & John Centre** is a one-stop shopping complex in the centre of Tsilivi which includes exchange facilities, post office, public telephone, travel agency, supermarket, car hire, swimming pool and a bar for cool drinks and snacks. ⓐ Tsilivi centre ⓣ 26950 42684

TAKING A BREAK

Balcony £ The Balcony hotel restaurant is perched on a cliff overlooking Tsilivi beach, and serves a variety of Greek *mezedes*, pizzas, snacks and ice cream. ⓐ Zakynthos Town road ⓣ 26950 28638 ⓦ www.balcony-zakynthos.gr ⓛ 08.00–23.00

Freddie's Beach Bar £ A lovely beach bar and restaurant with snacks, breakfasts and cocktails. ⓐ Tsilivi beach ⓣ 26950 27480 ⓛ 09.00–21.00

Gelato Café £ Home-made ice cream served in a friendly atmosphere. Gelato also has milkshakes, crêpes, sandwiches and other snacks. ⓐ Main road ⓣ 26950 41177 ⓛ 10.00–24.00

Salt & Pepper £ Beside the Ark cocktail bar, this snack bar has great crêpes, waffles, pizzas and pasta. ⓐ Main road ⓣ 26950 28976 ⓛ 10.00–24.00

Boat House ££ Part of the Tsilivi Beach Hotel but open to everyone, this elegant wooden restaurant is a good place to relax over drinks or a snack. ⓐ Tsilivi beach ⓣ 26950 23109 ⓛ 08.00–24.00

Piero's ££ A family-run restaurant with Mexican and Greek specialities at reasonable prices. Children welcome. ⓐ Main road, Planos ⓣ 26950 27046 ⓛ 09.00–24.00

Popeye's ££ Tsilivi's most popular restaurant and pizzeria, with a large terrace overlooking the main square. Also serves excellent English and international breakfasts. ⓐ Main road, Planos ⓣ 26950 23981 ⓦ www.popeyes.gr ⓛ 08.00–01.00

Trenta Nova ££ Tasty Greek cuisine, pizzas and snacks served in an outdoor snack bar. ⓐ Main road ⓣ 26950 22490 ⓛ 09.00–02.00

AFTER DARK

Restaurants

Koukos £ This friendly and good-value option is one of Tsilivi's best eating spots, with international options and a lively Greek night. ⓐ Main road ⓣ 26950 49019 ⓛ 09.00–24.00

O Kalofagas ££ Just inland from Amboulla beach on the main road, this well-established fish taverna serves excellent *kalamari*, swordfish and octopus. Good wine and Greek music. ⓐ 3 km (2 miles) west of Tsilivi ⓣ 26950 62634 ⓛ 12.00–23.00

The Olde Vineyard ££ Typical open-air taverna near the beach offering traditional Greek fare and wine from the barrel. ⓐ Bouka beach road ⓛ 12.00–23.00

Romeo & Juliet ££ This Italian restaurant and pizzeria lives up to its romantic name – it's perfect for a special night out, with or without the kids. ⓐ Main road ⓛ 09.00–23.00

Georgio's ££–£££ Elegant Greek dining in Tsilivi. There's a range of *mezedes* well worth trying, and the salads are fresh and delicious. ⓐ Main road ⓣ 26950 27086 ⓛ 09.00–23.00

Nightlife

Enigma The only club in town is brightly lit with neon on the outside, and has great all-night house and dance parties. ⓐ Main road ⓛ 23.00–06.00

Magdalena's A cosy, buzzing cocktail bar with fun staff and delicious cocktails. When the time's right after a few drinks, there's dancing too. ⓐ Main road, Planos ⓛ 17.00–02.00

Alykes & Alykanas

Just 15 km (9 miles) from Zakynthos Town on the northeast coast, Alykes (pronounced 'Al-leek-ess') and Alykanas (pronounced 'Al-leek-ah-nas') are ideal family resorts occupying 3 km (2 miles) of golden sands which shelve gently into crystal-clear, shallow waters.

THINGS TO SEE & DO

The Vertzagio Popular Art Museum

Well signposted from Alykes, this museum contains a fascinating collection of rare farming artefacts from the mid-19th century. See the flourmill, olive press, traditional crafts and antique bedroom full of old lamps and furniture with descriptions annotated in English. Children will love the gentle donkeys and goats that roam in the courtyard.
ⓐ Pigadakia ⓣ 26950 83670 ⓛ 09.00–18.00 ⓘ Admission charge

TAKING A BREAK

Taj Mahal & Chinese Golden Dragon £ Delicious selection of Chinese and Indian food ⓐ Katastari road, north of Alykes ⓣ 26950 83957

Taverna Kaki Raki £ For typical and traditional Greek meals in a village atmosphere. Families welcome. ⓐ Pigadakia ⓣ 26950 83670

Asteria ££ Welcoming restaurant attached to waterfront hotel of the same name. Try the hearty English breakfasts or pancakes with maple syrup. ⓐ Alykes seafront ⓣ 26950 84059 ⓛ 09.00–24.00

Dionysos ££ Try *saganaki* or feta cheese as a starter followed by tasty *keftedes* (meatballs) for a traditional Greek meal, and wash it down with the local wine at this taverna. ⓐ Alykanas ⓣ 26950 83954 ⓛ 10.00–23.00

Maestro ££ Friendly, family-run pizzeria and taverna. ⓐ Alykes ⓣ 26950 83101 ⓦ www.montes.gr ⓛ 08.00–24.00

Palm Tree 2 ££ Jon, the English cook, conjures up some of the best budget food on the island at this unpretentious beachfront restaurant. There's a daily changing menu with healthy and surprising options. Well worth a visit. On the main street there is a Palm Tree cocktail bar too. ⓐ Alykes beach ⓣ 26950 83565 ⓛ 09.00–24.00

Paporo ££ Try an enticing range of cocktails before dinner and enjoy the fabulous views of the sunset at this welcoming restaurant. ⓐ Alykes main road ⓣ 26950 83053 ⓦ www.paporo.gr ⓛ 09.00–01.00

Paradosiako ££ This Greek taverna nestles beneath huge shady trees and offers a good selection of home cooking and local wine. ⓐ Alykanas–Zakynthos road ⓣ 26950 83412 ⓛ 09.00–24.00

Olympic £££ An upmarket restaurant without a terrace or beach view, but with a stylish harbour-themed interior, top-notch food and an excellent selection of wines. Perfect for a special night out. Reservations essential. ⓐ Alykes main road ⓣ 29650 83507 ⓛ 16.00–24.00 ⓦ www.olympicbar.com

AFTER DARK

Nightlife

Buca Bar A seafront bar built on top of an old coastal defence bunker – you can see the spot where the cannon stood under the glass floor. An excellent place to catch the evening breeze with a beer or cocktail. ⓐ Alykes beach ⓣ 26950 83053 ⓦ www.bucabar.gr ⓛ 09.30–03.00

Catacomves A large wine and cocktail bar, with good views over the town and a wine cellar with a shop beneath the house. ⓐ Alykanas main road ⓣ 26950 83362 ⓛ 10.00–23.00

Zakynthos excursions

BOAT TOURS

The Kianou Caves, at the northern tip of the island, are only accessible by boat. Kianou means 'blue' and you will understand why when you dip into the translucent blue waters that fill these magical sea grottoes. Boat trips from the major resorts also visit Shipwreck Bay, otherwise known as Navagio. This stunning bay is named after a cargo ship that is said to have come to grief on a smuggling mission, but that now lies half-buried in the sands beneath the sheer cliffs. Tour boats drop anchor here to allow passengers to enjoy views of the dazzling white cliffs and to take a dip in the clear waters. To take a short boat trip to the wreck from Port Vromi, follow the signs from Anafonitria, turning left at George's Tavern. If you want to see the beach and wreck from the cliff above, follow the signs for the viewpoint, where a platform enables you to take an unforgettable picture-postcard snapshot.

MONASTERIES & CRAFTS

The traditional handicraft village of Volimes, in the north of Zakynthos, is the place for those who enjoy browsing for rugs, lace, carpets, table linen and all sorts of crafts at bargain prices. Nearby is the Anafonitrias Monastery, where Aghios Dionysios, the patron saint of the island, spent his final years as abbot. Besides relics of the saint, the monastery has 15th-century icons and 17th-century frescoes.

Further south, Macherado has the most ornate Greek Orthodox church on the island. Aghia Mavra has a richly decorated interior and Venetian-style bell tower. Towards the end of the day, head for Kampi, on the island's west coast, to enjoy spectacular cliff-edge views of the sun going down over the Ionian Sea. The village has a small folk museum, but the big draw, without doubt, is a ringside seat in one of the two tavernas perched 300 m (985 ft) above the sea.

Gaios

Gaios (pronounced 'Guy-yoss') bustles with visitors who fill the waterside tavernas or pass the time of day watching the elegant boats in the harbour from the handsome village square. The capital, with its winding streets and whitewashed houses cascading with flowers, has a relaxed, easy-going atmosphere.

The town beach at Yiannos lies to the south of town and there's another fine sandy beach and turquoise waters at Mogonissi islet, easily reached by water taxi from Gaios.

THINGS TO SEE & DO

Paxos Museum

This small museum, now housed in a former school building, contains a reconstruction of a Paxiot home, old national costumes and artefacts.

Gaios harbour

The Island of Paxos

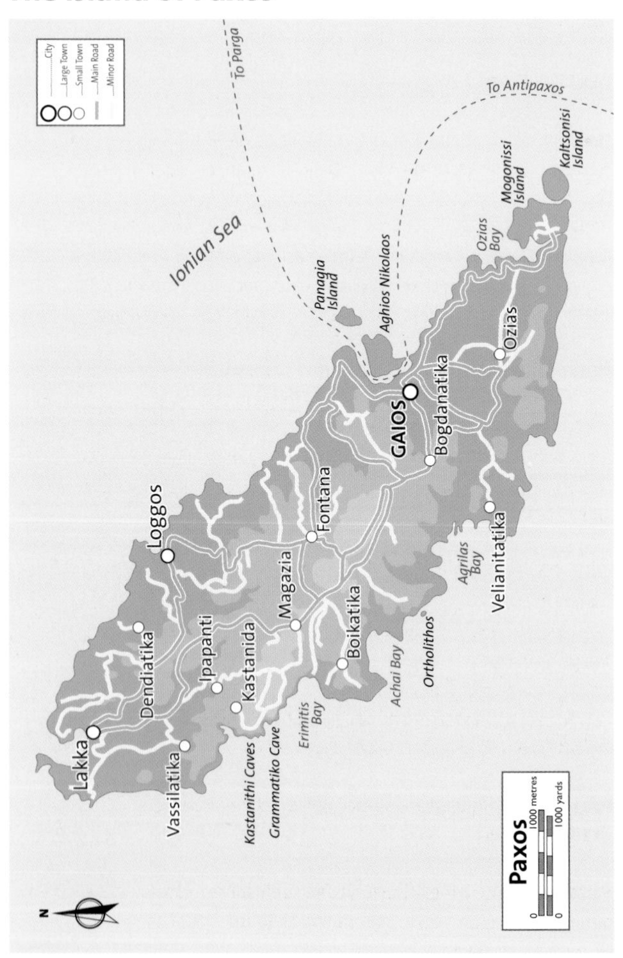

Waterfront 26620 32556 11.30–14.30, 19.30–23.30
Admission charge

TAKING A BREAK

The Cellar £ Great Greek fast food on the corner of the main square; *gyros, souvláki* and other snacks. Main square 26620 32263 11.00–02.00

George's Corner £ Corner fast-food snack bar offering burgers and *mezedes*. Good streetside location in lively part of the town. North side of the main square 26620 32362 09.30–02.00

Anneta ££ Sit beneath gaily patterned awnings and enjoy excellent fish and grills. Waterfront 26620 32670 09.30–23.00

O Faros ££ Fish, grills and Greek specialities can be enjoyed in this comfortable outdoor taverna and bar. Popular with holidaying Italians and yachties from Corfu. Waterfront 26620 31345 09.00–24.00

Genesis Bar ££ Great cocktails and good music with views of the wooded islet of Aghios Nikolaos opposite and the statue of local 19th-century war hero, Yiorgos Anemogiannis. Waterfront 26620 32495 10.00–01.00

Pan & Theo ££ Pastas, pizzas and fresh fish with waterside views. Waterfront 26620 32458 08.30–01.00

Petrino ££ Fashionable music bar. Next door to George's Corner 26620 32025

Volcano £££ Fine wines, fine food and sophisticated atmosphere in this family-run taverna beside the church. South side of the main square 26620 32251 09.00–01.00

Loggos

This small resort has a pebbly beach to the north of the village. Even more laid-back than Lakka, it sees fewer visitors but livens up during the holiday season. Small fishing boats bob in the harbour backed by the tiny village and an abandoned olive oil and brandy factory. A short walk south through wooded headlands of olive groves and pine trees leads you to the white pebble beach of Levrechi.

TAKING A BREAK

Evopi Snack Bar £ Small and cosy with a special selection of coffees and delicious ice creams. Or try a cool beer and enjoy picturesque views of the harbour. ⓐ Waterfront ⓣ 26620 31711 ⓛ 11.00–24.00

Loggos's harbour is in a natural horseshoe-shaped bay

O Gios ££ A simple but popular fish taverna – daily catch of octopus and squid. Fine selection of wines. Informal atmosphere. ⓐ Waterfront ⓣ 26620 31735 ⓛ Open for lunch and dinner, 12.00–01.00

Gonia ££ With a cornerside location, this family-run taverna serves traditional Greek meals and is so photogenic that artists come to paint the scenic surroundings. ⓐ Waterfront ⓣ 26620 31060 ⓛ 09.30–23.00

Nassos ££ Seafood is this taverna's speciality but grills are also served. For pleasant and panoramic views of the harbour, there's a separate upstairs terrace. ⓐ Waterfront ⓣ 26620 31604 ⓛ 12.00–24.00

Taverna Vassilis ££ Close to the town beach, this family-run taverna has seating outside in a pretty flower-filled alleyway. ⓐ Waterfront ⓣ 26620 31587 ⓛ 09.00–23.00

Olive Tree ££–£££ Signposted from the harbour, this tiny taverna has romantic tables with green chequered tablecloths in a pretty alley. The imaginative menu lists fresh fish, Mediterranean dishes and specialities like Bloody Mary soup. ⓐ Loggos village ⓣ 69728 52043 ⓛ 11.30–24.00

MUSIC FESTIVAL

Every year, in late summer, Loggos is the rather surprising venue for the Paxos International Music Festival when young artists from all over Europe arrive to study and perform in the old school house. These concerts are very popular and are attended by famous musical personalities, who act as artistic directors. Look out for posters advertising the venues or see your rep.

Lakka

Lakka (as in 'lacquer') lies on Paxos's northern tip, and its picturesque harbour surrounded by verdant hills attracts yachting groups and people in search of peace and quiet. The island's oldest church stands nearby, and from a ruined windmill you can see Corfu. Three small, pebbly beaches provide good snorkelling, waterskiing, windsurfing, sailing and scuba diving, or you can relax in a good choice of tavernas and bars. South of Lakka is the white-pebble beach of Malathendri, where the fish are so friendly they literally eat out of your hand.

THINGS TO SEE & DO

Aquarium Lakka

Over 100 species of fish from local waters are displayed in 27 tanks. The display changes every year but expect to see moray and conger eel, octopus and lobster.
ⓐ On the Gaios road near the bus stop ⓣ 26620 31389 ⓛ 10.00–14.00, 18.30–21.00 ⓘ Admission charge

TAKING A BREAK

Klimataria £ Famous for Eccles cakes baked by the English proprietor. If you're missing home, try the cottage pie. Features outdoor seating under a grapevine in the smaller of the two village squares. ⓣ 26620 30075 ⓛ 12.00–24.00

Fanis ££ Comfortable seating in this waterfront café with views of fishing boats. Ask for the Greek doughnuts, which come freshly cooked and oozing with honey. ⓐ Waterfront ⓣ 26620 31939 ⓛ 09.00–01.00

La Rosa di Paxos £££ Upmarket dining on flower-filled terrace on the waterfront; Italian specialities and fish. Fine selection of wines. ⓐ Waterfront ⓣ 26620 31471 ⓛ 12.00–23.00

Paxos excursions

Antipaxos

The beaches here are said to rival those of the Caribbean so, unsurprisingly, Antipaxos attracts hundreds of day-trippers. But to see Antipaxos at its very best, take an evening excursion from Gaios when the crowds have gone and enjoy a swim at Voutoumi beach. Stop at the 7th-century church of Aghios Emelianos to see its displays of fine paintings or visit the small settlement of Vigla, where vineyards flourish and fruit orchards burst with pomegranates, figs and apricots. There is only one taverna at Voutoumi beach and another high above the beach with exquisite views. Sea taxis to Antipaxos depart regularly from Gaios, Loggos and Lakka, taking about 15 minutes. Simply let the captain know when you want to be picked up again.

Northern villages

Paxos is a walker's paradise best explored by taking a guided walk following goat and mule tracks which wend their way past sleepy villages. On the way you can visit the island's only Byzantine church at Ipapanti, the stunning cliffs of Kastanida, and stop for refreshments at a Venetian stone mansion at Vassilatika near Lakka.

Parga

Excursion boats leave for Parga (see page 89), a charming coastal village on the Greek mainland. Parga has good in-town and nearby beaches, and makes a great base for trips to the ruins of Nekromanteion (see page 92), believed by the ancients to mark the Gates of Hades, located at the end of a lovely cruise down the Aherondas River.

Sea caves

Paxos's west coast is rugged with high cliffs and magnificent sea caves which can only be discovered by boat. Many people take excursion boats from Gaios to visit the impressive 183-m (600-ft) high caves of Kastanithi, the monolith-fronted Ortholithos, and the biggest cave, called Grammatiko.

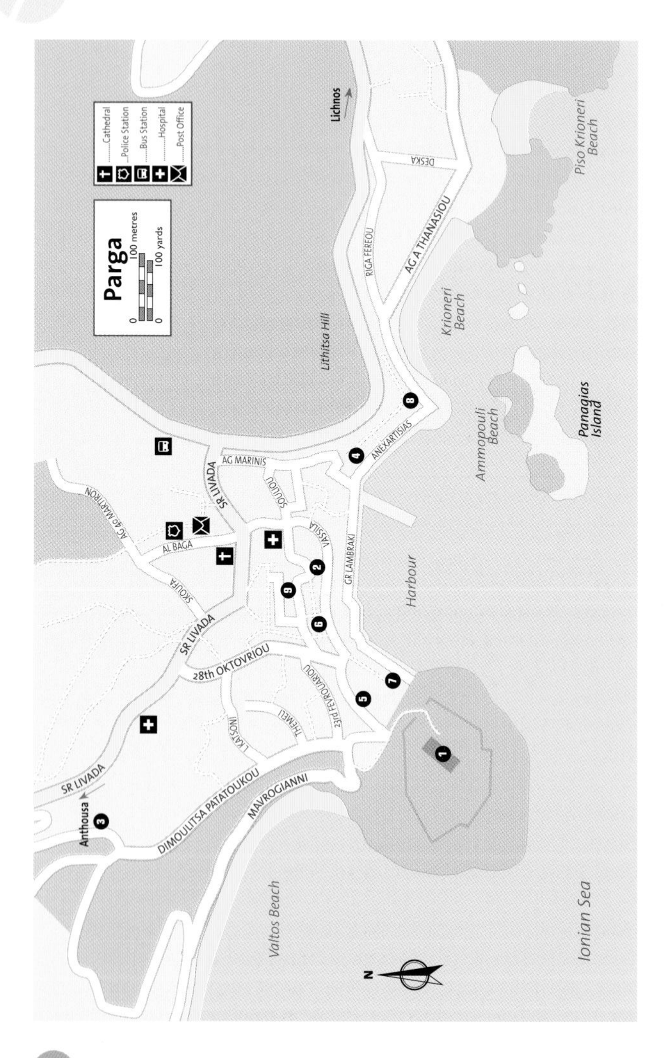
Parga
0
100 metres
0
100 yards
Cathedral
Police Station
Bus Station
Hospital
Post Office
Lichnos
Anthousa
Lithitsa Hill
Harbour
Valtos Beach
Ionian Sea
Krioneri Beach
Piso Krioneri Beach
Ammopouli Beach
Panagias Island
SR LIVADA
DIMOULITSA PATATOUKOU
MAVROGIANNI
28th OKTOVRIOU
23rd FEVROUARIOU
THEMELI
L KATSONI
SKOUFA
AL BAGA
AG 40 MARTIRON
AG MARINIS
SOULIOU
VASSILA
GR LAMBRAKI
ANEXARTISIAS
AG A THANASIOU
RIGA FEREOU
DESKA
N

Parga

Parga (pronounced as it is written) is a charming and atmospheric village set in a large bay on the Greek mainland, backed by mountains clad in olive groves and stands of green pine. As the main resort for the Epirus region of northwestern Greece, Parga is a busy holiday town, with plenty of life, but one where the traditional Greek way of life has not been spoiled by tourism. **International Travel Services** (ⓐ 4 Spyrou Livada ⓣ 26840 31833 ⓦ www.parga.net) is an established travel agency that offers advice and arranges local excursions, rentals and accommodation.

Parga's bustling harbour is lined with restaurants, bars and nightspots, while behind is a labyrinth of narrow, cobbled alleys lined with traditional red-tiled houses, stretching up to the Venetian fortress. This massive fortress, known as the Kastro, was built in 1572 on the site of a building destroyed several times before. The fortress commands fine views over the harbour and out to the rocky islets scattered across the bay.

Parga's attractions include cruises southwards along the coast to the mouth of the **River Acheron**. The ancient Greeks believed this was the **River Styx** – the river that souls had to cross before entering Hades – where legend has it that swimming in its waters makes you look 20 years younger. You can also visit the turquoise waters of Aphrodite's Caves.

BEACHES

Krioneri & Piso Krioneri

These two small beaches lie within walking distance of Parga Town. Umbrellas and sunbeds are available for hire.

Lichnos

Clean, quiet and lying in a deep, tree-clad bay, Lichnos attracts day-trippers who arrive in water taxis from Parga Town. You can waterski from the watersports centre right on the beach and learn the techniques of wakeboarding. Tavernas and restaurants provide snacks and meals. Lichnos lies 3 km (2 miles) southeast of Parga Town.

Valtos

Parga's best beach, Valtos, consists of a 1.5-km (1-mile) stretch of pebble and sand just beyond the Venetian fortress to the southwest. The beach is reached by a 20-minute stroll through olive groves from the town centre, or by water taxi from Parga Harbour (every 30 minutes from 09.00). Facilities include windsurfing and parascending.

THINGS TO SEE & DO

Tourist train

Go on a two-hour trip up into the hills to visit Anthousa village and Ali Pasha's castle, which offers magnificent views of Parga and the coast.
ⓐ Departs from the harbourfront ⓣ 69457 93049 ⓑ Daily at 10.00, 12.00 18.00 & 20.00

Valtos, Parga's best beach

Watersports

There's waterskiing, paragliding, wakesurfing, pedalo rental and more at Watermania (t 69447 68403) on Valtos beach.

TAKING A BREAK

Café inside the Castle £ ❶ Well worth the trudge up to the castle. Here you can sit in the shade of fragrant pine trees with beautiful views over town while sipping coffee or drinking cocktails. a Parga Castle t 26840 31150 w www.pargaweb.com/castle-cafe 09.30–02.00

Eden £ ❷ An American-run bistro serving pasta, ice cream, healthy sandwiches, home-made cakes and both sweet and savoury crêpes. a 26 Vassila t 26840 31409 10.00–01.00

Oasis £ ❸ Lovely garden setting away from the bustle of Parga. Take your pick from what's on offer, from delicious *tiropittakia* (cheese pastries), fried courgettes and aubergines. a Village centre, Anthousa, 3 km (2 miles) from Parga t 26840 31396 09.00–23.00

Sugar Bar £ ❹ Sit outside and enjoy a coffee looking out over the beach. With its extensive range of cocktails, this is also a great nightspot. a On Parga's central waterfront w www.sugarbar.gr 10.00–03.00

Blue Bar ££ ❺ Enjoy your cocktails, fancy ice creams and drinks in this lively bar near the castle. a On the way to the castle at the top of the steps at Gaki Zeri t 26840 32067 18.00–03.00

AFTER DARK

Restaurants

Taka Taka Mam £ ❻ Original Greek taverna and cuisine in street setting. Take your pick from the kitchen. Very good *stifado* and wine from the barrel. a 11 Alexandrou Baka t 26840 32286 10.00–23.00

Shanghai £–££ ❼ Two carved pillars with roaring dragons mark the entrance to this Chinese restaurant at the castle end of the bay. The large menu has many affordable options, with plenty of fish dishes. ⓐ Waterfront ⓣ 26840 32501 ◔ 17.00–24.00

Dionysos ££ ❽ One of the oldest tavernas in town, serving up good portions of delicious fresh fish and other Greek specialities. ⓐ Waterfront ⓣ 69451 43793 ◔ 09.00–24.00

Castello £££ ❾ Highly regarded and upmarket courtyard restaurant, forming part of the Acropol Hotel, located 150 m (165 yds) from the harbour. ⓐ Aghios Apostolon 4 ⓣ 26840 31833 ◔ 18.30–24.00

PARGA EXCURSIONS

The Nekromanteion of Efyras (Gateway to the Underworld) and Kassopi

The **Oracle of Nekromanteion** (built c. 3rd century BC) is where ancient Greeks communicated with the dead. ⓐ 22 km (14 miles) southeast of Parga, near the village of Mesopotamos ◔ 08.00–19.00 (summer), 08.00–15.00 (winter) ❗ Admission charge. Further south are the remains of **Kassopi**, a town built in the 4th century BC. In 1803 a group of local women committed suicide here, close to the Zalongo monument, rather than surrender to the approaching Turkish army. ⓣ 26810 41026 ◔ 08.30–15.00 Tues–Sun ❗ Admission charge

Preveza

A lively waterfront and location of the region's main airport but also noted for the extensive ruins of the city of **Nikopolis**, just 7 km (4 miles) to the north. Preveza is located 65 km (40 miles) south of Parga. The ruins and museum are open to the public. ◔ 08.30–15.00 Tues–Sun ❗ Admission charge

---

▶ *Boat trips are available all over the Ionian Islands*

LIFESTYLE
Island life

Food & drink

THE GREEK TAVERNA

The Greek taverna is a wonderfully flexible institution. You are made equally welcome whether you just want to settle down with a beer and a plate of chips or Greek salad, or whether you arrive with a group of friends to sample a *mezedes* feast.

Some tavernas have an extensive menu featuring everything from simple grilled chicken to fresh fish sold by the weight. Others have no formal menu: the waiter will tell you what is available or, better still, you will be invited into the kitchen to view the range of prepared dishes and daily specials on offer. You place your order by pointing to the dishes you want. If you do order prepared food, do not be disappointed if the moussaka or stuffed tomatoes are served lukewarm – this is the traditional Greek way, and the food will usually be reheated if you ask.

A typical Greek dish

STARTERS

Many Greek starters are now familiar to everyone through the products sold on supermarket shelves throughout Europe, but every taverna has its own recipe or its own style of presenting such typical dishes as *taramasaláta* (smoked cod's roe beaten with potatoes, lemon juice and oil) and tzatziki (yoghurt dip with cucumber and garlic).

More unusual dishes to look out for are *gigantes* (fresh butter beans cooked in tomato sauce), *melitzanosaláta* (aubergine dip, sometimes served with tomatoes), *arakas* (peas in herb dressing), *dolmadákia* (vine leaves stuffed with herb-flavoured rice) or *saganaki* (grilled or fried cheese). Typically, a Greek salad (*saláta horiátiki*) will consist of lettuce, onion, cucumber, tomatoes and olives with a chunk of feta (crumbly white sheep's milk cheese) on top – almost a meal in itself.

MAIN COURSES

Taverna staples include *moussakás* (minced lamb layered with potatoes, aubergines and white sauce) and *kleftiko* (lamb with herbs, baked in foil in the oven until it is meltingly tender). Minced beef, lamb, pork or veal can be used to make spicy meatballs called *soutsoukakia* (sausage-shaped) and *keftedes* (round), often served in tomato sauce. *Pastitsio* (sometimes called *pasticio*) is a delicious layered pie made from minced meat, macaroni, tomatoes, cheese and white sauce, reflecting Venetian influence on Greek cuisine.

Stifado is the term for any casserole; though usually made from veal, each island has its own variations on this Greek staple, which can also be made from rabbit or tender chunks of beef, cooked long and slow with herbs, vinegar, tomatoes, onions and garlic. Grilling over a wood or charcoal fire adds a special flavour to chicken, *souvláki* (skewered cubes of pork or veal, flavoured with oregano), *kalamari* (squid) or *barbounia* (red mullet). As a concession to visitors, some tavernas serve doner kebab (*gyro* in Greek), though this spit-roasted meat, served in pitta bread with salad and sauce, is traditionally sold from specialist fast-food stalls rather than restaurants.

Fresh fish can be the most expensive dish on the menu, but the price is worth paying for a special night out – most restaurant menus will

state whether the fish is fresh or frozen, and the price should reflect this, with frozen *garides* (prawns), for example, being a third of the price of fresh ones. If you like fish but do not want to spend a fortune, go for *marides* – whitebait – for a delicious and inexpensive meal.

VEGETARIANS

Greek restaurants make good use of seasonal fruit and vegetables, and if you get to know the taverna owner, they may well prepare something just for you, given a day's notice – meat-free stuffed tomatoes or peppers, for example. Among dishes found in many tavernas, look for *briam* (similar to ratatouille, and made from aubergines, peppers, courgettes and tomatoes); *melitzanes fournou* (baked aubergines – usually made with onions and tomatoes); *fassólia* and *bamyes* (green beans and okra, respectively, cooked in a herb-rich tomato sauce); and *kolokithea tiganita* (courgettes fried in batter).

DESSERTS

Greeks go to a *kafeneion* (café) or *zacharoplasteio* (pastry shop) if they want sweet desserts, though tavernas have adapted to visitors to the degree that they may well offer fresh fruit, fruit salad, ice cream or a velvety smooth dish of yoghurt and honey. At a café, the choice of pastries is much wider: look for *baklava* (filo pastry, honey and nuts); *kadaifi* (shredded wheat and nuts drenched with honey syrup); and *loukoumades* (honey and cinnamon-flavoured doughnuts). You will also

GREEK TAKEAWAY

Greek fast food is designed to fill that hole that develops mid-morning or at any time of day when you are on the move. Bakers and kiosks sell little pies made from filo pastry and deliciously filled with cheese (*tiropitta*), spinach (*spanakopitta*) or minced lamb (*kreatopitta*). For sweet lovers, there is *bougatza*, bursting with delicious vanilla custard, or apple-filled *milopitta*.

find nougat and *halva* (a dessert made from sesame paste, honey and nuts) on offer.

DRINKS

Retsina is the best-known Greek wine, and you will find it on the wine list everywhere you go in Greece. Flavoured with pine resin, it is a taste that, once acquired, can become addictive. If you prefer something truly local, ask for house wine, which will be served to you in a jug, often drawn direct from a large barrel. These wines are so cheap that you can experiment, and most of the time they will be pleasant and refreshing. Two other drinks are commonly served in Greek cafés. *Ouzo* has a strong aniseed taste, which you will either love or hate – try it with ice and water, or with lemonade or fresh orange juice. *Metaxa* is Greek brandy, and the higher the number of stars (3, 5 or 7), the better the quality. You could also ask for the drier *kamba*.

Sun-ripened local produce is cheap and plentiful

Menu decoder

Here are some of the authentic Greek dishes that you might encounter in tavernas or pastry shops.

Dolmadákia Vine leaves stuffed with rice, onions and currants, dill, parsley, mint and lemon juice

Domátes/piperiés yemistés Tomatoes/peppers stuffed with herb-flavoured rice (and sometimes minced lamb or beef)

Fassólia saláta White beans (haricot, butter beans) dressed with olive oil, lemon juice, parsley, onions, olives and tomato

Lazánia sto fourno Greek lasagne, similar to Italian lasagne, but often including additional ingredients, such as chopped boiled egg or sliced Greek-style sausages

Makaronópita A pie made from macaroni blended with beaten eggs, cheese and milk, baked in puff pastry

Melitzanópita Pie made from baked liquidised aubergines mixed with onions, garlic, breadcrumbs, eggs, mint and parmesan cheese

Melitzanosaláta Aubergine dip made from baked aubergines, liquidised with tomatoes, onions and lemon juice

Mezedes A selection of appetisers, such as tzatziki, *dolmadákia* and *melitzanosaláta*

Moussakás Moussaka, made from fried slices of aubergines, interlayered with minced beef and béchamel sauce

Pastítsio Layers of macaroni, parmesan cheese and minced meat (cooked with onions, tomatoes and basil), topped with béchamel sauce and baked

Píta me kymá Meat pie made from minced lamb and eggs, flavoured with onions and cinnamon and baked in filo pastry

Saláta Aubergine dip made from baked aubergines, liquidised with tomatoes, onions and lemon juice

Saláta horiátiki Country salad (known in England as 'Greek salad'); every restaurant has its own recipe, but the basic ingredients are lettuce, tomatoes, cucumber, onions, green peppers, black olives, and feta cheese dressed with olive oil and oregano

Souvláki Kebab usually of pork cooked over charcoal

Spanakotyropitákia Cigar-shaped pies made from feta cheese, eggs, spinach, onions and nutmeg in filo pastry

Taramasaláta Cod's roe dip made from puréed potatoes, smoked cod's roe, oil, lemon juice and onion

Tỳrópita Small triangular cheese pies made from feta cheese and eggs in filo pastry

Tzatziki Grated cucumber and garlic in a dressing of yoghurt, olive oil and vinegar

THE KAFENEION

In Greek villages, the *kafeneion* (café) remains very much a male preserve, although visitors of both sexes will be made welcome. Customers come here to read the paper, debate the issues of the day and play backgammon, as well as to consume *elinikos kafés* (Greek coffee). This is made by boiling finely ground beans in a special pot with a long handle. Sugar is added during the preparation rather than at the table, so you should order *glyko* (sweet), *metrio* (medium) or *sketo* (no sugar). In summer, try *frappé* (iced coffee).

Shopping

Tourist shops in the Ionian Islands open all hours, including Sundays, and they accept credit cards for all but the smallest of purchases. Local shops have more restricted hours and are usually closed over lunch, and all day Sunday. You may want to shop in local shops and markets for some typically Greek souvenirs, such as worry beads, or – if you have fallen in love with the lively tones of bouzouki music – some music CDs featuring your favourite Greek melodies. Other typically local goods include honey, nougat, dried herbs, cheeses, olives and decorative ceramic pots.

FASHION

In the island capitals of Lefkas Town, Zakynthos Town and especially Argostoli, there is a good range of boutiques selling both international and modern Greek designs. Sometimes you see replica designer items such as Calvin Klein sweatshirts, Levi jeans and Joop handbags sold at a fraction of their usual price; be careful to examine the goods carefully for quality before you buy these.

JEWELLERY

Greece produces many excellent designs in gold and silver, and the prices for handmade earrings, rings, bracelets, medallions and necklaces are very competitive compared to the cost of mass-produced jewellery sold back home. Gold is graded in carats, from 14 (the cheapest) up to 24, and silver is graded according to its purity, 1000 being pure silver. Designs range from the ultra-modern to copies of ancient Greek jewellery.

LEATHER

Another Greek speciality, leather goods are of exceptional quality and workmanship, and competitively priced. Treat yourself to a purse, wallet or handbag, or buy school satchels for the children or some sandals for the beach.

Twilight shopping in Argostoli

RUGS & TEXTILES

So many hours of hard work go into the production of hand-woven carpets and embroidered tablecloths or cushion covers that you would not expect them to be cheap. Even so, if you see something you really like, buy it – because it will be considerably cheaper here, bought direct from the producer, than from a shop or department store back home.

Children

BOAT TRIPS

Children love boat trips. Interesting excursions are available from Nidri (see pages 22–3) and Vassiliki (see page 24), or from Zakynthos Town to the National Marine Park (see box page 62) or Shipwreck Bay (see page 80). Better still, get together with some other parents and charter a boat – if there are a number of you it will not cost a lot. You can decide with the owner where to go – seek out some small private cove and play at being stranded on a desert island for the day.

Boat trips are ideal for playing at pirates for the day

EATING OUT

Greek families eat out together, so your children will be welcome in the local taverna, where they will probably make friends with other children, despite the language barrier. Most restaurants catering for tourists have a children's menu featuring such favourites as chicken, pizza, beefburgers or fish fingers, and quite a number have a play area. Children in Greece stay up late at night, made possible by the afternoon siesta – a habit you might want to emulate to avoid the midday heat.

EXCURSIONS

Kids will love to scramble around the ruins of the Turkish castles of Parga (see page 89) or St George's Castle on Kefalonia (see page 53), but keep a close eye on them as dangerous parts are not fenced off. Tourist trains in Zakynthos Town (see page 57) and Parga (see page 90) offer gentle trips to neighbouring villages that can be fun for younger children.

SPORTS & PASTIMES

Facilities vary greatly from resort to resort. Horse riding is available at several resorts. There are also go-karting tracks on several of the islands, often combined with mini-golf courses so that there's something to do for both speedsters and slowcoaches. Your hotel, any travel agent or the tourist office can tell you more about what's available in the area.

WATERSPORTS

Older children who are confident swimmers will love the range of watersports on offer. The Lefkas resort of Vassiliki is famous for windsurfing (see page 24), but this is also available at Parga's best beach, Valtos (see page 90), and also at Tsivili (see page 75) on Zakynthos. For excellent snorkelling, try Agiofili (see page 25) on Lefkas or Skala (see page 48) on Kefalonia. Diving centres will be happy to take older children on trial dives. Younger children will be delighted with the glass-bottomed boat tours available at many resorts, and several beaches also have pedalos for hire, which offer an opportunity to explore the clear inshore waters, looking for fish and loggerhead turtles.

Sports & activities

ENJOY YOURSELF ON LAND & SEA

The island resorts are all well supplied with facilities for sports, including tennis and mini-golf. You can also choose from a growing range of watersports that will test your skill and sense of adventure (be sure to check first, however, whether your insurance policy covers you).

Your best bet, if you want to try out windsurfing, sailing, paragliding, waterskiing or scuba diving, is to sign up for a training course with one of the watersports centres that are based in the main resorts. Top instructors will adapt their instruction to your level of competence, so even intermediate- and advanced-level tuition is available.

If the idea of watersports fills you with horror for whatever reason, seek out a beach where motorised sports are banned. There are many quiet coves where peace and quiet reign, and on Zakynthos most watersports are banned in the Laganas Bay area to protect the loggerhead turtles.

BELOW THE WATER

Warm, crystal-clear waters make the Ionian Islands a wonderful place to go diving. There are several schools where equipment can be hired and where a range of courses is available at every level, from beginners to experienced divers. If you're not sure, you can always join a half-day trial dive to see if you like it. Alternatively, try snorkelling or a trip on a glass-bottomed boat to get a glimpse of life below the waves.

WALKING & CYCLING

Walking and cycling allow you to adjust to the pace of real Greece, explore sleepy villages and archaeological sites, observe nature at close quarters, and get a better understanding of the agricultural way of life in Greece. You can hire mountain bikes in many resorts, and trail maps and information leaflets are available from some tourist offices. Two of the best areas to explore are the mountains of Lefkas and the east coast of Zakynthos (which, being flat, is also popular with cyclists).

Sign up for a windsurfing course on one of the islands

SUMMER FLOWERS

The Ionian Islands are renowned for their wild flowers, but you have to come in spring (March to June) for the best displays. In summer, you will see the hardy sea daffodil, with its sweetly scented white flower, which uses its huge bulb as a reservoir of food and water during the hottest months. Other plants flowering at this time of year are bougainvillea, with its thorny stems and purple flowers, pink-flowered oleanders and rock roses.

Festivals & events

There are two ways to get under the skin of Greek culture, both of them equally enjoyable. One is to attend a Greek evening and the other is to take part in a festival. Folk evenings can be artificial events put on for tourists, but on the Ionian Islands the music and dance you will experience during a typical Greek evening are part of a living culture. *Kantathes* (folk songs) still play a vital part in village festivals, and they can be heard all over the islands in tavernas where local people sing to entertain each other. Equally popular is the haunting mandolin-like melody of the bouzouki.

Festivals are common in the summer months when local people celebrate the name day of the patron saint of their church or monastery. These festivals, called *panayiria*, are religious in focus, but eating, drinking, music and dancing play a central role. Street vendors set up stalls selling local products and there is usually a barbecue selling delicious grilled foods.

EASTER

Zakynthos is one of the most festive of the islands, with a two-week carnival leading up to Shrove Tuesday, followed a few weeks later by the Holy Week celebrations. Greek Orthodox Easter can be anything from one to three weeks later than Easter in the Western calendar and so may coincide with your visit. This colourful celebration begins at midnight on Easter Saturday, when rifle shots are heard and fireworks light up the sky to welcome the news that Christ is risen. On the Sunday, lamb is roasted over great open-air barbecues, and eaten for lunch, with sweet cinnamon-flavoured Easter biscuits to follow, all washed down with bottles of wine from the previous autumn's vintage.

AGHIOS DIONYSIOS

The feast of Aghios Dionysios – better known as St Dennis, the patron saint of Zakynthos – is celebrated on 24 August. It is believed that St Dennis still walks the island and that his slippers wear out (see box

A religious icon from Zakynthos Museum

Traditional dancing

page 55), so they are replaced annually when the silver casket that holds his mummified remains is opened in August. St Dennis's body is then paraded around the town centre and harbour area. In the evening, a carnival atmosphere takes over the island. Market stalls are erected throughout Zakynthos Town and a procession is held to the sound of local bands and exploding fireworks.

Finding your way around is easy

PRACTICAL INFORMATION

Tips & advice

Accommodation

The Ionian Islands have hotels offering accommodation in all price ranges – the following is a brief selection. Price ratings are based on the double room rate with breakfast in high season:
£ below €75 **££** €75–150 **£££** over €150

LEFKAS

Lefkas Town

Patrai £–££ Housed in a pretty yellow and green building overlooking the lively main square. Rooms are clean and simple, and most have balconies. The quiet rooms are at the back. ⓐ Main square, entrance on Meganissou ⓣ 26450 22359

Vassiliki

Katina's Place £–££ Lovely family-run pension just behind the harbourfront with fully equipped studios as well as basic rooms. ⓐ Vassiliki village ⓣ 26450 31602 ⓦ www.katinasplace.gr

KEFALONIA

Argostoli

Olga £–££ A comfortable town-centre hotel directly on the waterfront promenade with views of the fishing boats and ferries. Good value for its simple and clean rooms. ⓐ 82 Paralia A Tritsi ⓣ 26710 24981

Lixouri

Apolafsi ££ Just outside Lixouri along the coast, this quiet and spacious hotel set between the olive trees has a large pool and is a short distance from several stunning beaches. ⓐ Lepada ⓣ 26710 91691 ⓦ www.apolafsi.gr

Sami

Athina ££ Just north of Sami in Karavomylos village, this pretty beach resort hotel is well placed for both sunbathing and trips to caves and beaches. ⓐ Karavomylos ⓣ 26740 22779 ⓦ www.athina-beach-hotel.com

Fiskardo

Regina £ A pleasant pink guesthouse overlooking Fiskardo from the hill behind the waterfront. Simple, clean rooms with fridge, air conditioning and balconies. ⓐ Upper village ⓣ 26740 41125

PAXOS

Gaios

Paxos Club ££–£££ Set in olive groves just outside Gaios, this resort hotel has spacious apartments overlooking the beautiful hotel pool. ⓣ 26620 32451 ⓦ www.paxosclub.gr

ZAKYNTHOS

Zakynthos Town

Yria ££ A good-value, modern hotel in the heart of town, with the central square and town beach just a short walk away. ⓐ 4 Kapodistriou ⓣ 26950 44682 ⓦ www.yriahotels.gr

Vassilikos

Koukis Club ££–£££ A beautiful resort hotel along Aghios Nikolaos bay beach. The rooms have good views and there are plenty of facilities for children. ⓣ 26950 35427 ⓦ www.koukisclub.gr

Laganas

Gloria Maris ££ Set on a promontory away from Laganas's nightlife area, this beachfront hotel has a pool and pleasantly shaded areas by the beach. ⓐ Laganas beach ⓣ 26950 51546 ⓦ www.gloriamaris.gr

Tsilivi

Tsilivi Beach Hotel ££–£££ On the edge of the resort, this large beachside hotel has balconied rooms. There's a good restaurant on site too. ⓐ Tsilivi beach ⓣ 26950 23109 ⓦ www.tsilivi-beach-hotel.gr

Preparing to go

GETTING THERE

The cheapest way to get to the Ionian Islands is to book a package holiday with one of the leading tour operators, often offering flight-only deals or combined flight-and-accommodation packages at prices that are hard to beat. The flight time from London is three to four hours. If you're staying on Paxos, getting there will involve a flight followed by a bus and ferry ride.

There are numerous charter airline companies offering flights to Greece during the summer months, although if you travel out of season, you may have to use a scheduled flight with British Airways (t 0870 850 9850 w www.ba.com) or Olympic Airlines (t 0870 60 60 460 w www.olympicairlines.com) to Athens and a connecting flight with Olympic Airlines to one of the Ionian Island airports. You can also choose to use one of many budget airlines flying to Greece; see w www.whichbudget.com for a complete overview of connections. If you can be flexible about when you visit, you can pick up relatively inexpensive special deals. As a rule, the further in advance you buy your ticket, the cheaper it usually is – but you can also get good last-minute deals from online travel agents via the Internet.

Many people are aware that air travel emits CO_2, which contributes to climate change. You may be interested in the possibility of lessening the environmental impact of your flight through the charity **Climate Care**, which offsets your CO_2 by funding environmental projects around the world. Visit w www.jpmorganclimatecare.com

TOURIST INFORMATION

In the UK, the Greek National Tourist Office (a 4 Conduit Street, London W1S 2DJ t 020 7495 9300 w www.gnto.co.uk e info@gnto.co.uk) can provide general information about visiting Greece, and has useful brochures and maps that you can download online or order. Many Ionian resorts that are popular with British tourists have inspiring websites made by long-term visitors.

BEFORE YOU LEAVE

It is not necessary to have inoculations to travel in Europe, but you should make sure you and your family are up to date with the basics, such as tetanus. It is a good idea to pack a small first-aid kit to carry with you containing plasters, antiseptic cream, travel sickness pills, insect repellent and/or bite-relief cream, antihistamine tablets, upset stomach remedies and painkillers. Suntan lotion and after-sun cream are more expensive in Greece than in the UK so it is worth taking some. Take your prescription medicines with you, as you may find it impossible to obtain the same medicines in Greece.

Although Greece is a very safe country when it comes to petty crime and has a good healthcare system, it's a good idea to purchase travel insurance before you go. Check the policy carefully regarding medical coverage, dental treatment, loss of baggage, flight cancellations, repatriation, etc., and whether activities like scuba diving, horse riding and watersports need extra coverage. If you are forced to seek medical help, keep all medical receipts for claim purposes; if your possessions are stolen, you'll also need to file a police report. UK visitors carrying a European Health Insurance Card (EHIC) get reduced-cost and sometimes free state-provided medical treatment in Greece and most other European countries. The free card can be ordered via the Department of Health (t 0845 606 2030 w www.dh.gov.uk).

ENTRY FORMALITIES

All EU citizens and citizens from all Western countries only need a passport to enter Greece. Visas are only required by certain nationalities; details can be found on the Greek Foreign Ministry website w www.mfa.gr. Check well in advance that your passport is up to date and has at least three months left to run after your return (six months is even better). All children, including newborn babies, need their own passport. It generally takes at least three weeks to process a passport renewal. This period can be longer in the run-up to the summer months. For the latest information on how to renew your passport and the processing times, contact the Identity & Passport Service (t 0870 521

0410 ⓦ www.passport.gov.uk). Check the details of your travel tickets well before your departure, ensuring that the timings and dates are correct. If you plan to rent a car in Greece, be sure to have your driving licence (and that of any other drivers) with you, including the photo card if you have one; carrying an international driving licence is not necessary.

MONEY

Like many EU countries, Greece uses the euro. Euro (€) note denominations are 500, 200, 100, 50, 20, 10 and 5. Coins are 1 and 2 euros and 1, 2, 5, 10, 20 and 50 lepta. At time of research, the exchange rate was £0.68 to the euro. The best way to get euros in Greece is by using your debit bank card in an ATM, which can be found in all towns, resorts and airports. Make sure you know your PIN and check with your bank to see if there are any charges for using your card abroad; Nationwide is the only UK bank offering free ATM transactions abroad. Credit cards are increasingly accepted in Greek resort hotels and restaurants, but less so in shops and supermarkets. Check the validity date and credit limit of your cards before you go. You can purchase cash euros before leaving the UK, but bear in mind that changing cash locally at a bank or exchange office will be much better value. Another very secure way of carrying your holiday money is to use a pre-paid currency card such as Thomas Cook's Cash Passport (ⓦ www.thomascook.com/cashpassport). You can pre-load these 'digital wallets' with as much cash as you like, and then either use the card like a debit card in shops and restaurants, or withdraw cash from ATMs using your PIN.

CLIMATE

July and August are the hottest months on the Ionian Islands, with maximum daytime temperatures sometimes rising higher than 40°C (104°F) – it's best to stay out of the sun from 11.00 to 15.00. June and September are slightly cooler, with daytime temperatures rarely exceeding 30°C (86°F). During late May and early October, it's still just about possible to swim, but the weather can be unpredictable, with temperatures rarely exceeding 25°C (77°F). In high season, pack some

EU STUDENTS
Admission to all state-owned museums and archaeological sites in Greece is free for schoolchildren and university students anywhere in the EU – so be sure to bring your student ID card along, as it can save lots of money!

light cotton clothes so you can cover up when you've had enough sun. Even during summer, temperatures can drop dramatically at night, so you should also bring at least one light jumper or jacket.

BAGGAGE ALLOWANCE

Baggage allowances vary according to the airline, destination and the class of travel, but 20 kg (44 lb) per person is the norm for luggage that is carried in the hold; check your ticket to see if the weight limit is mentioned there. Large items – surfboards, golf clubs and folding wheelchairs and pushchairs – are usually charged as extras, and it is a good idea to let the airline know in advance if you want to bring these. You are allowed only one item of hand baggage measuring 55 by 40 by 20 cm (22 by 16 by 8 in) plus any airport purchases, umbrella, handbag, coat, camera, etc. Note that security measures at both UK and Greek airports prohibit you from taking any sharp objects or any liquids and gels in your hand baggage, except liquids necessary for the flight and packed in containers no larger than 100 ml (3½ oz) inside resealable plastic bags. Read more about the security rules on your departure airport website.

During your stay

AIRPORTS

The airports on the Ionian Islands are small and often crowded, with overpriced food and drinks – make sure you arrive well before departure time and bring plenty of patience, drinks and snacks. It's just a short ride from Zakynthos and Kefalonia airports to the island capitals and main resorts. The nearby airport of Preveza on the mainland is used for reaching Lefkas. Public transport is patchy or non-existent from these airports, but taxis are readily available, and many rental car agencies have offices at the airports. Note that it's often cheaper to arrange car hire in advance, and that in high season cars can be difficult to come by without advance booking.

COMMUNICATIONS

The Greek national phone company, OTE, has public phones in all towns, villages and resorts which accept OTE phonecards and have English-language instructions. Some resorts have private coin-operated phone booths but these are usually very bad value. You can also make calls from many kiosks or from a *kafeneion* in smaller villages; these have a metering system and you will be told how much your call costs at the end. Using a €5 prepaid calling card (available at any kiosk) is the cheapest way to phone abroad. These can be used from any OTE public phone or hotel phone (dial a free local number, then follow the English-language instructions to enter your code and call the number you wish to reach).

Many tourists bring their mobile phones and use roaming to phone home. Check the charges carefully as this can be a very expensive way to phone home. If you're planning to phone often and want to be reached as well, consider buying a local Cosmote or Vodafone SIM card (available from many kiosks and mobile phone shops for a few euros) so you have a local number incurring lower costs.

Most post offices are open Monday to Friday 08.00–14.30, the main ones in the island capitals until 19.30 and on Saturdays too. Post boxes are bright yellow with a blue logo; at major post offices you will find two

TELEPHONING TO & WITHIN GREECE
All telephone numbers in Greece, whether landline or mobile phones, consist of 10 digits, and there are no additional city codes. To make a call within Greece, simply dial these 10 digits. To call to Greece from abroad or from your mobile phone while in the country, dial the international access code, usually 00, followed by Greece's country code 30 and the 10-digit local number.

TELEPHONING ABROAD
To call abroad from Greece, dial 00 followed by the country code (44 for the UK, 353 for Ireland, 1 for the US, 61 for Australia, 64 for New Zealand and 27 for South Africa) followed by the city code (minus the initial 0) and the subscriber's number.

slots: *esoterik* for local mail and *exoterik* for overseas. Outside the main towns they are not always emptied every day. Postcards can take up to two weeks to get to Britain, letters three or four days; if you want your postcards to arrive back home before you do, then put them in an envelope. Sending a postcard or letter abroad costs €0.62.

CUSTOMS

Greeks are usually very friendly to strangers, and you are bound to experience traditional hospitality in one way or another during your stay. Greeks rarely begin their evening meal earlier than 21.00, and usually take the whole family along, babies too. Children are generally allowed to wander around restaurants, even late at night.

DRESS CODES

If you are visiting churches or monasteries, you will not be allowed in wearing shorts or beach clothes; it is best to wear long trousers or a skirt and take a shirt or wrap to cover your shoulders. Some churches provide clothing for visitors to use. Topless sunbathing is officially forbidden but still common in some beach resorts; judge the situation carefully before stripping and causing upset.

ELECTRICITY

Greece has 220 V electrical outlets. You will need an adaptor plug for any electrical equipment you bring with you and these can be purchased at the local supermarkets or in the UK before you depart. At times in high season, there may be power cuts lasting at most two hours, but usually much less. It is important to realise that electricity is expensive in Greece, so be considerate and do not leave lights and air conditioning on in your room when you go out.

EMERGENCIES

The general emergency number for ambulance, police and fire brigade in Greece is 112.

There is tourist police in Zakynthos Town (t 26951 24483), Lefkas Town (t 26450 26450) and Argostoli (t 26710 22815).

The best medical care is found in the island capital hospitals (Zakynthos Town t 26951 49111, Lefkas Town t 26450 25371, Argostoli t 26710 24641), though there are good medical clinics with multilingual staff in towns and resorts throughout the islands.

There is a British Honorary Vice Consulate in Zakynthos Town (a 5 Foskolo t 26950 22906 w www.ukingreece.fco.gov.uk e zakynthos@fco.gov.uk). If you are staying on Lefkas, Paxos or in Parga, you may find it more convenient to contact the British Consulate on Corfu (a 18 Mantzarou t 26610 23457 e corfu@fco.gov.uk). If you are on Kefalonia, there is an Honorary Vice-Consulate in Patras, on the Greek mainland (a 2 Votsi t 26102 77329). Check with your holiday representative before contacting them, as they can only offer limited help in extreme emergencies.

GETTING AROUND

Driving conditions

Remember that in Greece you drive on the right. Always carry with you your driving licence, passport and any other relevant documents when driving, and ask for a map when renting the car. The road quality on the Ionian Islands is generally quite good, with only smaller roads and unsurfaced tracks requiring you to slow down to protect your wheel rims. The main roads leading to and from the main towns can get congested in summer, but otherwise it's usually peaceful. In high season beware of slow drivers, holidaymakers on quad motorbikes, farmers watering their olive groves, and traffic jams. Beware of illegal parking in the island capitals as the police are quick to hand out fines. Blue lines on the street indicate paid parking, yellow lines official services only, white lines are free parking.

If you are stopped by the police for a motoring offence you are expected to pay your fine on the spot (make sure you get a receipt if you do). If you do not pay, the police will remove the licence plates from your car, which you will then have to reclaim from the police station on payment of the fine. If anything like this happens, you should contact your hire company immediately.

Car hire & driving

Drivers need to be over 21 (25 in some cases) and have a valid driving licence. Car hire is available at all resorts and costs around €30–60 per day for a small car, depending on season and length of rental. Local rental companies in the beach resorts often have lower prices than the international companies in the main towns. Most rental cars are new and zippy small cars, and air conditioning is quite common. Open-top 4WDs are popular too but much pricier. Insurance is included in your car rental, but is sometimes not valid if you use non-asphalted roads, and check that it includes damage to the wheels, tyres and roof.

Public transport

Bus transport is limited, but reliable and cheap on the three main islands. Buses are usually air-conditioned coaches and run on time. Printed timetables can be found at the tourist offices and at the bus stations in the three island capitals, where you can also buy tickets in advance. When getting on in villages and resorts, you usually pay the conductor after getting seated.

Taxi

Taxis can be found at arrival points, major hotels and driving around the larger resorts. They're comparatively inexpensive to use, and prices for longer distances are usually fixed. There's a surcharge after midnight. Any hotel or restaurant will call a taxi for you on request.

HEALTH, SAFETY & CRIME

Healthcare

There are a number of private medical clinics offering a 24-hour service and with English-speaking doctors. Details are available at local pharmacies. You'll find that pharmacies often have English-speaking staff and are very helpful for minor complaints and illnesses. They operate a rota system for opening outside normal shop hours (especially at the weekend) and information about the duty chemist is displayed in each shop. Generally, both over-the-counter and prescription drugs purchased at pharmacies will be cheaper than in England. However, some, such as antibiotics, can be expensive. Homeopathic and herbal treatments and remedies are very popular in Greece and widely available. Personal hygiene goods are also to be found in supermarkets.

Food & water

Travellers who are not used to olive oil may experience minor stomach problems for a few days – olive oil is good for your health so it's worth getting used to it! Tap water is safe enough, but bottled water is widely available, cheap and tastes much better.

Precautions

Cooling breezes off the sea can mask the intensity of the sun's rays, which can burn you if deflected off sand or nearby water. You can even burn in the shade, especially if you have sensitive skin. If you drive a car with an open sun roof, keep your shoulders covered and wear a hat. The same applies if you are wandering around shopping. Keep covered up during the hottest part of the day and drink plenty of water to avoid dehydration.

Sea urchins are quite common in rocky coastal regions; if you step on one, the spines can be removed with tweezers. You should then douse the affected area with lemon juice or ammonia; you can buy ammonia 'sticks', which are also good for jellyfish stings, at pharmacies.

Mosquitoes can be a nuisance but are easily dealt with by burning insect coils or using an electric deterrent. If you want to avoid the attention of wasps, bees and hornets, just ensure that you do not leave food out, especially sweet or sticky food.

Safety & crime

Compared to most Western European countries, Greece is a very safe place, with hardly any petty or violent crime – in fact, it's mainly other tourists, and not Greeks, that you have to be wary of! A forgotten camera or wallet will most likely still be on the restaurant table when you return for it, and public drunkenness or violence is quite rare. Still, avoid temptation by leaving all valuables and documents in the hotel safe and carrying only what you need. Be wary of bag snatchers in busy resorts and towns, and leave your car empty when you park it. The police keep a low profile but invariably turn up when needed at motor accidents and crime scenes, and to deal with illegally parked cars. There are also tourist police, who speak several languages and are trained to help with problems faced by tourists.

During the last couple of years, occasional protests and strikes against the government's fiscal austerity measures have affected services throughout Greece, briefly causing inconveniences for the local population (and for some unlucky visitors). However, even though foreign travellers have experienced slight discomforts due to such situations, you should not expect to run into serious danger in Greece, where such shows of workers' solidarity are nothing new. Indeed, since any violent protests tend to target large banks, government buildings and global financial institutions in Athens (and sometimes Thessaloniki), tourists don't have much to worry about.

Restricted areas & photography

Greece has very strict rules about photographing any military installation. Army, navy and air force bases are surrounded with signs telling you not to take pictures. Civilian airports are often also used by the military, and taking photos there is forbidden too. It is also worth remembering that the 2001 case of British plane spotters in mainland Greece being tried for and convicted of spying was based not on photographs taken, but on information they wrote down in notebooks.

MEDIA

It's easy to stay in touch with home, as many resorts sell English newspapers, usually only a day or two out of date. Locally produced newspapers in English can be a useful source of information about local events. Most hotels with televisions and English bars have satellite TV for a dose of sports and news. The online English edition of Greece's *Kathimerini* newspaper is a good source of national news (W www.ekathimerini.com). There's also a section detailing festivals around Greece.

OPENING HOURS

Shops traditionally open from 08.00–14.30 on Monday and Wednesday, 08.00–14.00 and 17.00–20.00 on Tuesday, Thursday and Friday, and 08.00–13.00 on Saturday. Tourist resorts are a case apart and most shops open all day, usually from early morning until 23.00. Sunday is a general closing day, but shops serving tourism mostly remain open.

Banks are open 08.00–14.00 on Monday to Thursday and 08.00–13.30 on Friday. A few branches in the island capitals are also open from 09.00–13.00 on Saturday.

Restaurants are generally open 09.00–23.00. Breakfast ends around 10.00, lunch is usually between 13.30–15.30, and dinner starts late for Greeks – 20.00 is on the early side.

Churches are almost always open for visiting, but in villages you often have to find the lady in black who looks after the key.

RELIGION

Greece is dominated by the Greek Orthodox Church, with a faith that has strong historical roots in the local community. Saints' days and name days are very important celebrations. Weddings, baptisms and

A magical sunset dip on the spectacular beach at Myrtos on Kefalonia

funerals are serious and lengthy occasions. Be respectful and cover up before you enter a church or chapel.

TIME DIFFERENCES

Greece is in the Eastern European time zone, two hours ahead of the UK. Clocks go forward one hour on the last Sunday in March and back one hour on the last Sunday in September.

TIPPING

In restaurants a service or cover charge is often included in your bill. However, if the service warrants it, you can leave a small tip to the waiters or bar staff; 5–10 per cent is about right. Taxi drivers don't expect tips, but if you are happy with the service, give a tip. If you are shown around a church by the 'keyholder' or priest, a tip is also welcome, but this should always be left in the donations box rather than offered directly to the guide.

TOILETS

Public toilets are found in bus stations and main squares. Smarter facilities are found in bars, but you should buy a drink or ask nicely if you want to use them. Toilets are generally very clean, but you must observe the practice throughout Greece and not flush away used toilet paper. Do as the Greeks do and put it in a bin (provided in each cubicle) next to the toilet. Remember this, or you risk blocking the pipes!

TRAVELLERS WITH DISABILITIES

Greece is slowly catching up with the rest of the EU when it comes to facilities for the disabled. Many ramps have now been built on to beaches and in hotel and restaurant entrances, and some of the local buses have disabled access, but this is normally restricted to people on foot, not in wheelchairs. The island capitals are all flat and easy to get around. Some hotels have facilities for disabled people, but there are still very few taxis or buses that can cope with a motorised wheelchair.

ACKNOWLEDGEMENTS
We would like to thank all the photographers, picture libraries and organisations for the loan of the photographs reproduced in this book, to whom copyright in the photograph belongs: Archelon (page 63); Pictures Colour Library (pages 26, 74, 101); Jeroen van Marle (pages 10–11, 16, 38, 43, 45, 51, 65, 68, 72, 84, 90, 97, 102, 107, 109, 123); Thomas Cook Tour Operations Limited (pages 5, 13, 22, 24, 29, 58, 67, 93, 94, 105, 108); Dreamstime.com (pages 9 Straga, 49 Gary Dyson, 56 Garryuk, 81 Netfalls).

Project editor: Karen Beaulah
Layout: Donna Pedley
Proofreaders: Caroline Hunt & Jan McCann
Indexer: Marie Lorimer

Send your thoughts to
books@thomascook.com

- **Found a beach bar, peaceful stretch of sand or must-see sight that we don't feature?**
- **Like to tip us off about any information that needs a little updating?**
- **Want to tell us what you love about this handy little guidebook and, more importantly, how we can make it even handier?**

Then here's your chance to tell all! Send us ideas, discoveries and recommendations today and then look out for your valuable input in the next edition of this title.

Email to the above address or write to:
pocket guides Series Editor, Thomas Cook Publishing, PO Box 227, Unit 9, Coningsby Road, Peterborough PE3 8SB, UK

Useful phrases

English	Greek	*Approx pronunciation*
BASICS		
Yes	Ναι	*Ne*
No	Οχι	***O**-khee*
Please	Παρακαλώ	*Pa-ra-ka-**lh***
Thank you	Ευχαριστώ	*Ef-ha-ri-**sto***
Hello	Γεια σας	*Ya sas*
Goodbye	Αντίο	*An**dee**o*
Excuse me	Με συγχωρείτε	*Me si-nho-**ri**-te*
Sorry	Συγγνώμη	*Sig-**no**-mi*
That's okay	Εντάξει	*En-**ta**-xi*
I don't speak Greek	Δεν μιλώ Ελληνικά	*Den Mi-**lo** (E-li-ni-**ka**)*
Do you speak English?	Μιλάτε Αγγλικά;	*Mi-**la**-te an-gli-**ka**?*
Good morning	Καλημέρα	*Ka-li-**me**-ra*
Good afternoon	χαίρετε	***He**-re-te*
Good evening	Καλησπέρα	*Ka-li-**spe**-ra*
Goodnight	Καληνύχτα	*Ka-li-**nih**-ta*
My name is ...	Ονομάζομαι	*O-no-**ma**-zo-me*
NUMBERS		
One	Ένα	***E**-na*
Two	Δύο	***Di**-o*
Three	Τρία	***Tri**-a*
Four	Τέσσερα	***Te**-se-ra*
Five	Πέντε	***Pen**-te*
Six	Έξι	***E**-xi*
Seven	Επτά	*Ep-**ta***
Eight	Οκτώ	*Ok-**to***
Nine	Εννέα	*E-**ne**-a*
Ten	Δέκα	***De**-ka*
Twenty	Είκοσι	***I**-ko-si*
Fifty	Πενήντα	*Pe-**nin**-ta*
One hundred	Εκατό	*E-ka-t**o***
SIGNS & NOTICES		
Airport	Αεροδρόμιο	*A-e-rodromio*
Railway station	Σιδηροδρομικός εταμσς	*Sidirodromikos Stathmos*
Smoking/ non-smoking	Για Καπνιστές/ Για μη καπνιστές	*Ya kapnistes/ Ya mikapnistes*
Toilets	Τουαλέτα	*Tualeta*
Ladies/Gentlemen	Γυναικών/Ανδρών	*Yinekon/Andron*